MASTERCLASS: WRITING CRIME FICTION

Rosemary Rowe

Teach® Yourself

Masterclass: Writing Crime Fiction

Rosemary Rowe

First published in Great Britain in 2014 by John Murray Learning. An Hachette UK company.

First published in US in 2014 by The McGraw-Hill Companies, Inc.

British Library Cataloguing in Publication Data: a catalogue record for this title is available from the British Library.

Library of Congress Catalog Card Number: on file.

Paperback ISBN 9781473601369

eBook ISBN 9781473601383

10 9 8 7 6 5 4 3 2 1

Typeset by Cenveo® Publisher Services.

Printed and bound in Great Britain by CPI Group (UK) Ltd, Croydon CR0 4YY.

John Murray Learning policy is to use papers that are natural, renewable and recyclable products and made from wood grown in sustainable forests. The logging and manufacturing processes are expected to conform to the environmental regulations of the country of origin.

John Murray Learning
338 Euston Road
London NW1 3BH

www.hodder.co.uk

Also available
in ebook

To the late Dorothy Lumley, in grateful memory

Contents

About the author

Rosemary Rowe was born in Cornwall in 1942, but spent much of her early life in New Zealand. She is a graduate of Sydney and Wellington universities and holds a teaching diploma from Auckland as well as professional qualifications in drama, EFL teaching and educational management. Initially a teacher of English and languages in Taumarunui, New Zealand, she returned to England in 1967 and took up a teacher training post in Cheltenham, eventually specializing in English language teaching, a position which she held until 1987 when an industrial accident forced her to take early retirement. Now slightly disabled, she turned to writing, running writing courses and examining for Trinity College London. Under her married name of Rosemary Aitken, she is the author of a dozen Cornish historical romantic novels, more than a dozen language textbooks, a writing manual and several prizewinning poems and plays. She has also written light contemporary fiction and scores of short stories under different pseudonyms. However, she is probably best known for the Libertus series, crime novels set in Roman Britain featuring a Celtic pavement-maker sleuth, and written under her maiden name. Now divorced, retired and resettled in Cornwall with her partner, Rosemary has two children and five grandchildren.

Introduction

So you've decided that you want to write a crime fiction novel? Shrewd commercial choice! Hundreds of thousands of crime fiction books are sold worldwide each day, and there are avid fans. I hope you're one of them. But now you have decided that you want to write a crime novel yourself and have already shown that you are serious by picking up this book.

Writing Crime Fiction is designed to be specific to the field. What I have written is based on years of running a postal writing school and weekend seminars, tutoring a university 'crime writing' course, and also on my own experience as a crime writer. But you will also find advice from lots of other more famous authorities – look for the quotations scattered through the text. Of course, you don't want to learn to write like anybody else, you want to develop your own 'voice' and style – and only you can do that – but perhaps I can save you the time and effort you might otherwise expend having to learn lessons the hard way, from your own mistakes.

I hope to give you insights into how crime novels are different from other fiction genres and encourage you to experiment with specialist techniques, while also helping you to hone your general writing skills. I've put the chapters in an order that seems logical to me, but you do not have to follow it. This is not a book to read from cover to cover at one sitting if you hope to benefit. Dip into it – perhaps a little every day – and take time to digest one idea and try it out before moving on to the next.

Expect to work as you go. Each chapter contains a series of suggested writing tasks and related exercises. You needn't slog through them slavishly. Feel free to pick and choose. Do them in any order that you like. You might even want to repeat the helpful ones. This should be a voyage of discovery, not an irksome chore.

However, if a particular writing task does not appeal, I strongly suggest that you should still have a go. In crime writing in particular, going beyond your comfort zone can lead to new ideas. You may find, as others have, that the things you didn't want to do are those that teach you most. And please do keep copies of anything you write – at least while you are working through this book. You will need them later, as you will see below.

Here is an outline of what you can expect:

 Snapshot – a five-minute exercise or a series of questions to draw your attention to some concept or technique.

 Write now – a longer exercise where you are invited to write a page or two, usually something related to the topic of the chapter.

 Edit – a chance to rework and strengthen a piece of your own work. This is an essential skill – and the reason why you need to keep a copy of your work, especially if you are not very satisfied with it.

 Workshop – a piece of writing for you to think about, with guided questions on some aspect of technique. See below for a more detailed explanation.

 Key quote – what other writers have had to say about a topic.

 Key idea – the most important element to grasp.

Focus point – advice to take forward and apply to what you write.

Where to next? – this outlines what we're going to cover in the next chapter.

The workshop

This is a new kind of exercise, introduced especially in this Masterclass series. You will be offered an opportunity to look at a piece of someone else's writing, reflect on how it works (by answering a series of guided questions) and then compare it with something of your own – rather as if you were a member of a writers' group and were discussing skills. (Of course, if there is a real-life writers' workshop near to you, attending it would be an asset, too – but please, whatever other exercises you ignore, try at least to do the Workshop one.)

Finally in this section, here is a little tale.

There was once a fabulously wealthy Eastern prince whose riches had enabled him to fulfil all of his ambitions except one: having once seen a craftsman use a potter's wheel, he yearned to make a lovely hand-thrown pot. Accordingly he summoned the finest potter he could find, provided him with a studio within the palace walls, furnished it with the best equipment in the land and commissioned him to teach him how to throw a pot.

Flattered but nervous, the potter set to work. He began by throwing a demonstration pot, and was most impressed by the close interest which his pupil showed. Encouraged, he took his completed creation to the kiln and threw another piece of clay on to the wheel.

'Now, Your Highness, it's your turn to try. I'll stand beside you and instruct you as you go.'

The princeling shook his head. 'There'll be no need for that. I know now how it's done. Collect your fee from my steward as you leave. I'll throw my pot tomorrow. Thank you very much.'

Absurd? Of course. There are some things you cannot learn simply through observation or instruction. Writing is one of them. This book will guide you, but it is you who will 'make the pots'.

Snapshot exercise

Give yourself two minutes to write down the three most important things you personally feel you need to learn and hope to gain from this book.

This is your journey. I will do my best to give you signposts on the way. Let's begin by setting out some ground rules for the trip.

The rules for writing crime fiction

RULE 1: FORGET RULES

There is no set of rules that writers can follow to guarantee success. If there were, all authors would be millionaires. Besides, every writer does things differently. You have only to read a half-a-dozen best-selling books to realize this, which is both an inspiration and a curse. You have freedom, but will have to find the techniques, plots and characters that work for you. There is no fixed formula.

Even the rules for writing other novels – if there are any – often do not hold for crime. Take whodunnits, for example. We don't 'begin at the beginning, go on until you come to the end, then stop,' as the King of Hearts advised Alice to do in Wonderland. We begin with the end (the murder) and work backwards to find out how it occurred. The pivotal character (the corpse) cannot be revealed through action – which is the usual advice – since he or she is obviously dead. Normal rules don't necessarily apply.

RULE 2: THERE ARE NO OTHER RULES

This does not mean that there is nothing to be learned. There are some useful precepts that it is generally better to observe and certainly some pitfalls that new writers should avoid. There are successful authors who flout this advice and if you are hugely talented you may find that you can do the same. Most of us, though, find it easier to sell our manuscripts if we obey the conventions – to begin with anyway.

The three things every writer really needs to do

1 Persevere.

2 Practise.

3 Make time to read.

1 PERSEVERE

Learning to be a writer is largely about developing mental discipline. It requires not only an enquiring mind and being prepared to try new things, but also having the strength and stamina to stick with it to the end. It's not a job for quitters. There is a lot of toughness and patience required in settling to write, more still in editing.

Richard Bach

'A professional writer is an amateur who didn't quit.'

It also pays to be a realist. You write because you really want to write, not in the hope of gaining great reward. Even when all your work is done and you've found a publisher, great fame and fortune are unlikely to result – though, of course, these things are possible. Few writers actually make a decent living from their work. It is much more likely that – like the majority of authors – you will find that your royalties are not your bread and butter, but merely buy the jam, and that your real reward is seeing your name on the spine of a book that a stranger is reading eagerly.

2 PRACTISE

The only way to become a writer is to sit down and write – and I mean literally writing, not thinking about potential plots or planning characters.

William Goldman

'Writing is finally about one thing: going into a room alone and doing it.'

So, write. If you do not yet have an idea in mind (although you might well have one, since you are reading this), just make a daily appointment with yourself and write. Make it a very short appointment to begin with, if you like. Just five minutes first thing in the morning initially, perhaps, but try to fix the time and duration in advance – and write the first thing that comes into your head. Don't mess around with trying to rephrase, just write and try to keep going for the whole period that you promised yourself. (It may help to set a timer, if you have one, for your first attempts.)

Write

Here are some suggestions if you're stuck for an idea.

- Describe the room that you are sitting in, or the half-dozen things you should be doing next.
- Pick up a picture from a magazine and write a description of the scene or person that is depicted there.
- If all else fails and you still can't think of anything to write, try putting your frustration about that into words.
- Rant against your spouse. Or boss. Or anyone. Don't worry if you find you're writing vitriol. No one is going to see your ravings except you. (Disguise the name if you have any doubts.) In fact, writing a tirade against what 'gets to you' is a very useful exercise for would-be crime writers. Frustration and anger are powerful motives, after all, and if you have tapped those feelings now you can revisit them later when you need them for your characters.

For now don't worry about the quality of the writing – just get used to writing something every day. It doesn't really matter what implement you use: pencil, pen, computer – anything will do. (Some people prefer a pencil because you can rub it out, which is perhaps a reason for not using one. A pen is portable. But you're going to have to use a keyboard when you submit your manuscript, so there's something to be said for getting used to typing as you think.)

Be sure that you keep your early scribblings and exercises, though. If you're not using a notebook, put them in file or in a box. But do keep them. You will need them when we come to editing. Later, we will move on to working on your narrative daily. For now the important thing is that you keep your appointment with yourself. Then you can call yourself a writer, 'somebody who writes'.

 ## Walter Mosley

'The first thing you have to know about writing is that it is something you must do every day.'

3 MAKE TIME TO READ

This is almost as important as making time to write. Read anything: read classics, read rubbish, read humour, read noir, above all read the kind of book you are hoping to produce. If a particular author doesn't please you, ask yourself why not. Even more important, try to work out what it is about your favourites that you enjoy.

Reading is a part of every writer's repertoire. Not because you want to borrow other people's plots or steal their characters, but because you can observe their techniques in action – and then you can not only borrow these but take them home and practise them until they are your own. Or, conversely, leave them well alone.

 ## Stephen King

'I am always chilled and astonished by the would-be writers who ask me for advice and admit, quite blithely, that they "don't have time to read." This is like a guy starting up Mount Everest saying that he didn't have time to buy any rope or pitons. [...] If you don't have time to read, you don't have the time (or the tools) to write. Simple as that.'

Focus point

A writer is somebody who writes, who reads and has the capacity to persevere.

Where to next?

If you're going to be a 'crime writer', you will be writing 'crime'. But what is that, exactly? The classification is so wide that it covers everything from the ultimately gentle 'cosy' (including some that actually feature cats or dogs as detectives) to the darkest noir, with graphic scenes of sexual torture. There are mysteries and there are crime thrillers. Obviously, your first decision will be to choose what part of this spectrum you hope to occupy.

So let's begin our journey with an examination of the scope of 'crime'.

1

Exploring the genre

What is crime fiction? As we shall discover in this chapter, there is a no single answer and even the classic types of this richly diverse genre – from whodunnit to howdunnit to whydunnit – can be broken down into subdivisions or their boundaries blurred. What matters, though, is that we should care about the characters involved and that there is real jeopardy – which means that there must be violence, usually murder, at the heart of the story.

What is a crime fiction novel?

This may seem self-evident but it is worth defining in our terms. A crime fiction novel is:

- **a novel** – which means a full-length book. You should aim at somewhere between 60,000 and 90,000 words. Any shorter and it becomes more of a novella or long short story, which are different markets. Any longer and it will be very difficult to sell. (However, even as I write, a crime story of over twice that length has just won the Booker Prize. In this game there are no absolutes.) But 60,000 or so words will give your book the greatest chance. When (and if) you find a publisher, your editor will guide you as to cuts – or even which parts of your story to expand.

- **fiction** – which means you're going to make it up. There is an entirely different market for non-fiction crime. Of course you may use real-life events, or even characters, as inspiration; everybody does. But as inspiration only. The final story comes out of your head – not out of research and newspapers. And since you have possibly never seen a corpse, much less a murder, you are simply going to have to imagine it.

Key idea

General advice to aspiring novelists is to 'write about what you know'. Unless you are a murderer, police officer, advocate or judge, this won't apply to the central incident in crime novels. This is the first of the 'general rules' that we are going to break.

Even so, there are no absolutes. There is a sort of 'half-fact' variety, in which a purely fictional character re-examines a famous actual event – usually one that happened long ago. (There are also examples where this pretends to be the case but the supposed distant murder is imaginary too.)

And this brings us to the special requirements of the genre.

The four central requirements of the genre

1 The novel is about a crime – preferably murder.
2 This crime is the driving force behind the plot.
3 The crime will out and justice will be done.
4 The author will 'play fair' with the reader.

1 IT IS ABOUT A CRIME – PREFERABLY MURDER

This is the one essential requirement and so important that it must be said again. Your crime must be one with huge physical stakes for the victim. Usually this is murder, although kidnap, violent rape, torture, child abduction and horrific cruelty to animals have all been used, though mostly in crime thrillers, rather than mysteries.

Howard Haycraft

'There really must be a murder, or at least a major felony – otherwise, what's the point? Who's ripping off the hand towels at the Dorchester Hotel is hardly the business of a mystery novel.'

Don't try basing a crime novel on a theft of art or jewels – unless there is a murder in the course of it. Some great writers (Agatha Christie and Conan Doyle) have done it, but not in full-length books. This is the stuff of short stories. For a whole novel mere theft is not enough, even when fabulous treasure is involved.

In particular, don't base your book on dreadful doings at banks or companies, however much that's 'writing what you know'. If you want to air that subject, try a different genre: a factual exposé or social satire perhaps. Financial double-dealing does not stir the blood. It won't create enough tension to sustain a crime novel – unless there is a murder, and not often, even then.

Key idea

There must be very high physical stakes for the victim for a crime novel to work.

Read through the following:

> She looked at the police officer with anguished eyes. 'My baby,' she whispered, as though it cost her pain to speak. 'Only three weeks old. She was right here. I put her down myself.' She shook her head. 'I left the room a moment – only a moment – because I thought I'd heard someone at the door but when I came back in here she had disappeared!'

1   Ask yourself: what is your attitude to the woman in the extract? Think of three adjectives you might apply to her.

2   Now reread the extract, substituting the words 'diamond necklace' for 'baby' (and 'it' for 'her', where appropriate) and repeat the exercise.

Which alternative feels like 'high stakes' for the woman?

2 THE CRIME IS THE DRIVING FORCE BEHIND THE PLOT

This does not mean that you are limited and cannot tackle psychological, social or political issues. On the contrary, these may be compelling triggers for a homicide – and sometimes the most chilling butcheries of all are those committed in the name of an idea. Just ensure that the human drama is what drives the narrative. This applies even when the central crime does not actually occur – in psychological thrillers, for example. Here it is the threat or suspicion of the crime that propels the narrative, whether or not it actually happens.

3 THE CRIME WILL OUT AND JUSTICE WILL BE DONE

The conventions of the genre generally require that good overcomes evil in the end, or at least that the lesser of two evils wins. This does not mean that every loose end must be neatly tied up and all peripheral questions answered, as was the fashion once. Nor does 'justice' necessarily imply the force of law. In fiction written when hanging was the law, a female or sympathetic criminal was often permitted to escape the noose, for instance by committing suicide. In novels set in other periods (or countries) whose forms of legal punishment seem particularly cruel, a different kind of justice may have to be invoked, so that the punishment seems commensurate to modern Western eyes.

Jean-Patrick Manchette

'The crime novel is the great moral literature of our time.'

Write now

Give yourself a quarter of an hour. Write down as many motives as you can think of for committing murder. Be as specific as you can. Don't write 'love' or 'jealousy', write something like 'Jo abandons her partner Henry and takes up with Fred.' Free your imagination and let your mind run wild – just keep writing until the time is up. Try to fill at least a page with different ideas.

Important note

If you are already part way through a crime novel, you may add that motive to your list of course, but *please* do not use what you have already written as the basis for these exercises, until we come to the point where that is suggested. This is because you will already have made decisions about settings, character and plot and this book hopes to teach you new approaches and techniques. Try them out first, and don't apply them to your major opus till you're familiar with them.

---

4 THE AUTHOR WILL 'PLAY FAIR' WITH THE READER

This means that all information necessary to solve the crime (or the rescue in a thriller) should be made available to the reader at the same time as the sleuth. It may be hidden or disguised (we'll look at methods later) but it must be there. It should be possible for perceptive readers to work out the solution for themselves – for many this is the whole attraction of the genre.

Given these general requirements, you have enormous scope. There are so many varieties of crime novel, and so many subgenres, that it would be impossible to list them all. However, it might be useful to look at some of the major categories, so here are some suggestions of examples you might read, if you are unfamiliar with a particular type of crime writing.

The main varieties of crime fiction

There are two major divisions of crime writing, either of which may occur in the 'specialist bracket'. So we shall look at:

- **crime mysteries,** including whodunnits, howdunnits and whydunnits
- **crime thrillers,** including psychological thrillers.

In addition, there are **specialist** genres, which may be either of the above, but add something extra, in particular historical crime, exotic crime and comic crime.

These distinctions are arbitrary of course, and there are recognizable subgenres within all of them. But it may be helpful to do a swift analysis and look at the advantages and disadvantages of each, including what makes them hard to sell or easier to write.

 Key idea

Whodunnits are not the only kind of crime novel. Work out which varieties most appeal to you.

CRIME MYSTERIES

As the term suggests, these are the stories that focus on a puzzle to be solved. They fall broadly into three categories:

1 Whodunnits (which has distinct subdivisions of its own)

2 Howdunnits, and

3 Whydunnits.

Whodunnits

These are still by far the most widely written and read of all varieties of crime fiction, so much so that many recognized subgenres exist. They differ chiefly in focus, setting, the nature of the sleuth, the tone of the writing and the amount of graphic violence in the text. All, however, have a basic similarity.

- **Focus:** on the puzzle and the mechanics of the crime, which is almost always murder – often more than one.
- **Sleuth:** may or may not be a professional, but is intelligent and/ or resourceful.

- **Solution:** arrived at through the application of that intelligence or resourcefulness (not accident or chance).
- **Cast of suspects:** a group of people, any of whom may have done the crime for different reasons, is an essential element of the genre.
- **Setting:** may be anything. The nature of the setting often sets the genre.
- **Motives:** range from the purely personal to political and social motives. There may be more than one person with motive, or no apparent motive for anyone at all (though there *will* be one – this is not the genre for writing about random killers or psychopaths).

Here are the most important subdivisions of the genre.

THE CLASSIC 'DETECTIVE' NOVEL

Willard Huntington Wright (S.S. Van Dine)

'There simply must be a corpse in a detective novel, and the deader the corpse the better.'

- **Focus:** the puzzle and the cleverness of the sleuth. The plot is usually complex.
- **Sleuth:** may be a police officer but more commonly a private detective or an amateur. There is often a secondary 'Watson' figure, with whom clues and theories can be discussed.
- **Solution:** arrived at by the application of intelligence. Depends on clues – often a matter of noticing apparent trivia and slight discrepancies in the testimony of different witnesses.
- **Cast of suspects:** outwardly respectable people, often interlinked, not all of whom are necessarily pleasant characters. Driven to murder by old-fashioned passions like jealousy and greed.
- **Setting:** may be country or city, but a generally law-abiding, ordered world. Sometimes a confined environment – such as the classic 'country house' – thus limiting the possible suspects.
- **Tone:** intelligent and sometimes literary. The degree of explicit violence is usually not high. Generally the criminal, when identified, confesses rather than, for instance, attempting violence.

Examples: almost any writer from the so-called 'Golden Age'. Try Agatha Christie's Poirot novels, Margery Allingham, Dorothy L. Sayers, Edmund Crispin or the earlier exponent, Arthur Conan Doyle.

May suit you if you like a puzzle and enjoy creating motives and red herrings and disguising clues. This form is probably the easiest to plot. It has a natural structure (as we will later see) which gives automatic shape to the book.

Not for you if you dislike a middle-class and 'literary' tone or seek gritty modern realism in what you write. It can seem dated, especially if set in the present with a 'sleuth' who is not a professional, as amateurs aren't permitted near a scene of crime these days.

'COSY' CRIME WHODUNNITS

- **Focus:** the hidden tensions in a village or rural society.
- **Sleuth:** almost always a private individual, often a woman, with some professional role giving her access to the whole community (though probably not as doctor, magistrate or police officer).
- **Solution:** often hinges not only on clues (as above) but on understanding the personalities and dynamics of the community.
- **Setting:** pivotal. A rural or village setting – or, rarely, a very small town – but generally a peaceful law-abiding place.
- **Cast of suspects:** as in the classic form. Not all the characters are wholly likeable (adultery and snobbery are common themes), though there is generally only one real 'bad egg' to be unmasked. Motives are often complex and purely personal.
- **Tone:** typically fairly gentle, descriptive and genteel, and the degree of violence generally small. Though grisly corpses may be discovered, we rarely see anyone being killed.

Examples: Agatha Christie's Miss Marple novels, M.C. Beaton (the Agatha Raisin books), Rebecca Tope, Carola Dunn. Often the title will tell you it's a 'cosy crime' (e.g. *Knit One, Kill Two* by Maggie Sefton). Or try the ultimate, the cat detectives of Vicky Halls, Linda Stewart or Carole Nelson Douglas (to name just three of the 40 or so exponents of that type of tale).

May suit you if the 'genteel' tone suits your style and you know a real semi-rural location fairly well (like the Cotswolds or West Virginia). It's important that you can portray this sympathetically, while hinting at tensions behind the bland façade. Pacy writing is a requisite as there is rarely violent action to speed the plot along. Good plots and lively characters are pivotal. This genre may seem a bit old-fashioned at a glance, but is still being written and has ardent fans.

Not for you if you seek a realistic, gritty modern tone. The rural tone is difficult to catch if you're a city dweller.

POLICE PROCEDURALS

- **Focus:** the battle of the police officer against crime in general and this one murder in particular.
- **Sleuth:** a member of the police, investigating the crime in the course of duty. Has modern methods and technology at his or her disposal – but is subject to modern constraints on interrogation methods. Must be a rounded personality, with faults as well as gifts, and not a cipher in a uniform. Typically a maverick who does not always do things by the book.
- **Solution:** arrived at by patient police work, including fingerprints, interrogating suspects and witnesses – often assisted by a team. May involve the work of specialists (e.g. forensics and ballistics – see Howdunnits later on). Often a colleague does the boring work of searching computer bases.
- **Setting:** usually larger towns or cities, sometimes fictional.
- **Cast of suspects:** the public – and not always the most savoury specimens. The police officer naturally knows a group of criminals, who may or may not be involved as part of the plot or subplot.
- **Tone:** professional and sometimes world-weary. Moving into more generally 'realistic' realms. (The police officer is accustomed to the seamy side of life and understands that people don't always tell the truth.) Bad language and violence don't come as a surprise. The degree of violence is moderate to high. There may be graphic descriptions of corpses, wounds and physical struggles – including gun and knife fights. Deaths may happen 'on the page'.

Examples: Ian Rankin, Michael Connelly, Ed McBain, John Creasey, Georges Simenon.

May suit you if you are an organized thinker with a gift for characters, know a town or city very well and have some understanding of what police procedure is (or are prepared to research this with great care). It will require you to know a great deal about, for instance, how fingerprints and DNA are checked, yet call for restraint in how much of this appears. The goal is to create the illusion of reality, while keeping the story moving but not making factual mistakes. Generally fictional police officers are not allowed to fight or strike a suspect except in self-defence.

Not for you if systems and teamwork don't appeal or you don't like research.

- **Focus:** gritty realism in a clearly modern world.
- **Sleuth:** a world-weary private eye (or citizen, in some varieties) who becomes embroiled with serious criminals.
- **Cast of suspects:** generally the urban underworld, including nightclub and casino owners, criminals, pimps and prostitutes.
- **Solution:** often relies on confrontation, including violence. The police are as likely as anyone to be corrupt or physically aggressive. The sleuth may be required to shoot someone, in the course of 'justice'.
- **Setting:** a city, usually a run-down area of town.
- **Tone:** generally cynical but often with a snappy style. The degree of violence is generally high, as many of the characters are armed.

Examples: Raymond Chandler, Dashiell Hammett, Mickey Spillane, Sue Grafton, Walter Mosley. This is the archetypal 'hard-boiled' school, originating in mid-twentieth-century America.

Paul D. Brazill, Ray Banks, Tony Black, Allan Guthrie and Charlie Williams write 'Brit-grit', a modern British version of the same, featuring grim inner-city settings where police are powerless, and gangs, thugs, terrorists, hard gangsters, loan sharks and debt collectors rule. The sleuth is often a con-man himself (so that, like the Americans, he has a gun) now working on the side of greater justice. Fast-moving and hard-hitting, with a high degree of explicit violence.

Patricia Highsmith, Russell James and Stieg Larsson write 'noir crime', which is similar to 'hard-boiled', except that the protagonist is not a professional sleuth, but a loner – a suspected person, an investigating journalist or even an intended victim – battling the system. The outcome is often a compromise, or a 'lose–lose' situation.

There is currently a strong trend of Nordic noir. Apart from Larsson, try Henning Mankell's Wallander mysteries, Åke Edwardson, Helene Tursten, Arnaldur Indriadson, Anne Holt or Jo Nesbø.

May suit you if you want a 'modern' feel. Great if you are good at writing lively action in hard-hitting prose and know enough about the seamier side of city life (or are prepared to do enough research on it) to make it leap out of the page. It requires enough knowledge to describe wounds and physical fights (including gun and knife fights). Demands the ability to write crisp, fast-moving prose, create memorable characters and sustain the tension and the pace. This genre is probably the easiest of all to sell – at present, anyway.

Not for you if you are not attracted by ballistics, physical action and the criminal underworld. Not for the squeamish.

Here are three short crime-plot scenarios. Into which 'whodunnit' genre do you think each would best fit?

1 A petty thief discovers that a work of art he stole from a van disguises a priceless masterpiece belonging to a gangland millionaire, who demands it back with menaces. But before the painting can be returned, it disappears again and the body of the gangster's son is found in the thief's flat.

2 A man out gathering wild mushrooms discovers half a hand emerging from a pile of decomposing leaves. Further investigation leads to the discovery of an entire dismembered corpse – recently murdered, but conclusively identified (by the teeth) as a young woman who disappeared five years earlier.

3 A dotty ageing spinster moves into a house she recently inherited from a relative. On the first morning, when she goes downstairs, she is appalled to find a body on the kitchen floor – a young man who has obviously been strangled. Having no telephone she cycles into town to report this to the police. But when they return to investigate there is no sign of a corpse, no one has been reported missing, and she cannot convince anyone of what she saw.

Howdunnits

These are still puzzles, but here the prime factor in finding the solution to the crime is the murder method itself. There are two chief subdivisions.

THE 'LOCKED-ROOM' MYSTERY

This is so-called because, in the original version of the form, a newly dead corpse is found locked into a room, where all the keys are on the inside of the doors and all the windows fastened from within. The term is now generally used for 'impossible' crimes, especially in a confined environment.

- **Focus:** how a seemingly impossible crime was carried out.
- **Solution:** working out the method (which may be technical). Finding that identifies the criminal.
- **Sleuth:** may be a professional, but often an amateur with the knowledge and intelligence to solve the conundrum.

- **Cast of suspects:** complex, secret motives are not a requisite. Sometimes the likely killer is quite evident, but circumstances seem to prove the suspect innocent. It is up to the author to prove otherwise.
- **Tone:** much as a classic 'whodunnit'. The degree of violence is not often great, though in some modern examples it is explicit.

Examples: *The Three Coffins* by John Dickson Carr; *Murder on the Orient Express* by Agatha Christie.

May suit you if you are sufficiently ingenious to come up with a genuinely different version of the plot. It is essential that your solution works, and does not flout the laws of physics or of science (though characters may fear a non-human or alien agency). There is still a market for this type of mystery.

Not for you if technical puzzles do not appeal.

FORENSIC FICTION

Here the 'howdunnit' element is of a different kind. Modern science is used to work out where and how the victim met their end.

- **Focus:** modern science – usually forensic expertise, though psychological profilers are also possible.
- **Solution:** science leads to the discovery of the murderer.
- **Sleuth:** not usually a sleuth at all, though there is often a police officer as a 'sidekick' in the plot. The protagonist (who can be, and often is, a woman) has a life and personality outside the lab and may be in conflict with colleagues or authority.
- **Cast of suspects:** the general public, only whittled down by science.
- **Setting:** often much action takes place in a laboratory.
- **Tone:** brisk and professional, occasionally wry. Graphic descriptions of wounds and bodies are common in this genre.

Examples: Patricia Cornwell, Jack Hyland (forensic science), Val McDermid's Tony Hill series (psychology).

May suit you if you have expertise or an interest in pathology, psychiatry or at least medicine. A burgeoning market if it interests you.

Not for you if you have no real knowledge of the sciences involved. (Other 'expert witnesses', such as ballistic specialists, may contribute to the solution of the crime, although they are generally not the main protagonists. However, if that is your field of expertise ...)

Write now

Look at the three scenarios from the Snapshot exercise again, and remind yourself into which subgenre you decided each would fit. Then write an opening paragraph suitable for each one, paying attention to the setting and the tone.

Whydunnits

Less puzzle-oriented than other mysteries, whydunnits are concerned not so much with the solution to the crime as with understanding what was in the killer's mind.

- **Focus:** less on clues and methods, more on the psychological reasons for the crime (which has usually, but not always, already taken place – in which case further crimes are often planned). The intention here is to get inside the mind of the killer, who may or may not be criminally insane.
- **Sleuth:** usually the police, or victim's family. There may be a psychologist or profiler at work – sometimes even as protagonist.
- **Solution:** arrived at by coming to understand the mentality – and predicting the behaviour – of the killer.
- **Setting:** may be anywhere but most often modern, urban areas.
- **Cast of suspects:** varies. We may know who the killer is from the outset, or simply share their thoughts without knowing which of the characters they are. The killer is often mentally disturbed or a 'terrorist' dispassionate in pursuit of an idea. Often believes that they are acting perfectly appropriately. May be a serial killer.
- **Tone:** high in tension. Sometimes features a high degree of on-stage violence, including torture and extremes of sexual crime, before the criminal is stopped.

May suit you if you are interested in psychology (psychological profiling in particular) or understand psychotic behaviour from a medical or nursing standpoint. The genre allows for a wide choice of settings, characters and crimes and has a modern and realistic feel. The ability to write dispassionately, when in the killer's mind, is requisite. Good market prospects.

Not for you if are more interested in action than psychology. The degree of knowledge required cannot be bluffed.

Key idea

The 'serial killer' story has been popular as I write, but is hard to handle unless the reader is made to care about one victim in particular – in which case it becomes a 'thriller' of a sort. Which brings us to our next topic.

CRIME THRILLERS

Key idea

Mysteries are concerned with solving crimes, thrillers with attempting to prevent them happening.

These are the absolute reverse of the whodunnit. There is no mystery. No cast of suspects. There may or may not be a sleuth at all. The author lets the reader know from the outset about a threatened outrage, always violent (typically abduction followed by murder, rape or something similar), and reveals not only who is planning it but, crucially, who the intended victim is. Tension is therefore present from the start, especially when we know what the victim doesn't know.

- **Focus:** the intentions of the would-be criminal, and usually the mind of the intended victim, in parallel.
- **Solution:** this crime (which must look almost certain to succeed until the last minute) is not exactly solved, but thwarted by some daring act, or some intelligent breakthrough, by those confronting it.
- **Tone:** increasing pace and tension. Usually there are two points of view involved, which may be very different in character and tone. Generally the genre majors on suspense – the threat of violence rather than the act – but there may be violence in the final struggle scene. Sometimes there are preliminary crimes which do succeed – and which may include quite graphic death and torture scenes.

Focus point

In a thriller, the drama is in making the reader feel that things are evolving in the worst way possible.

David Morrell

'Traditional mysteries appeal primarily to the mind and emphasize the logical solution to a puzzle. In contrast, thrillers strive for heightened emotions and emphasize the sensations of what might be called an obstacle race and a scavenger hunt.'

May suit you if you are good at writing both suspense and action. Has built-in tension, but needs good plot twists to succeed. Requires great skill as tension must be maintained throughout. There are often not many characters, so strong characterization and the ability to 'put yourself in someone else's mind' are paramount. Does not require expert knowledge. Always topical. Not difficult to sell.

Not for you if you prefer a puzzle to writing for suspense, or have difficulty with plot twists and shifts of mood.

Snapshot exercise

This is a quick imagination exercise. Go back to the three scenarios from earlier again. What would have to change to turn any one of them from a whodunnit into a thriller? Jot down your ideas. What difference would that make to your suggested opening?

SPECIALIST GENRES

In addition to the classifications we've been looking at there are specialist genres, which may include novels from any category, from whodunnits to thrillers, but add an extra ingredient to the plot. Three of the most common specialist genres are:

- exotic crime
- historical crime
- comic crime.

'Exotic' crime

We have already mentioned Nordic noir, but there is a thriving market for stories (from all subgenres above) where a lively exotic setting adds interest, dictates the characters and types of crime, and often contributes to the mood and style. This may be for you if you know another country very well indeed.

Examples: Alexander McCall Smith (Botswana), Tana French (Ireland), David Hewson (Rome).

Historical crime

Here the choice of setting is unlimited – in any land and any century. There is one great advantage of writing in this genre: unless you set the story in the recent past, your readers won't have experience of the period themselves and modern technologies like DNA and fingerprinting will not constrain the plot. Do make sure, however, that you know enough about your chosen period not to make mistakes. Take time to do meticulous research. There will be experts out there, and they'll be watching you.

Examples: Stephen Saylor (ancient Rome), Rosemary Rowe (Roman Britain), Ellis Peters or Michael Jecks (medieval England), Anne Perry (Victorian England).

Comic crime

Any of the listed varieties (even the noir) can and do exist in some kind of humorous form. There is even an annual award for the best comic crime. The humour can range from biting wit and savage satire to the hilariously absurd, from the gently mocking to the side-splitting.

Examples: Jonathan Latimer (screwball noir), Lindsey Davis's Falco (historical crime with a witty edge), Mike Ridley (wry historicals), Donald E. Westlake's 'crime capers' or the Fethering series by Simon Brett (parody of classic crime).

If you can pull it off, there is a market here. A little humour is a wonderful leaven in any crime novel – even if only a witty exchange of dialogue. However, do not let it interfere with tension or interrupt the plot.

Workshop

Here is the opening of a crime novel:

Murder was like magic, he thought. The quickness of his hand always deceived the eye, and that was how it was going to stay. He was like the postman delivering to a house where afterwards they would swear there had been no callers. This was the knowledge that was lodged in his being like a pacemaker in a heart patient. Without the power of his magic he'd be dead. Or as good as.

He knew just from looking at her that she would be the next. Even before the eye contact, he knew. There had always been a very particular combination that spelled perfection in his thesaurus of the senses. Innocence and ripeness, mink-dark hair, eyes that dance. He'd never been wrong yet. It was an instinct that kept him alive. Or as good as.

He watched her watching him, and under the urgent mutter of the crowd, he heard echoing in his head the music. 'Jack and Jill went up the hill to fetch a pail of water...'

Val McDermid, *Wire in the Blood*

1 What kind of crime novel do you think that this will be? Make a list of all the clues that you can find that tell you this.
2 Who do you think 'he' is? Victim? Killer? Sleuth? What do you know about him after these three paragraphs? What has the author done to make you feel uneasy about him?
3 Who do you think 'she' is? What do you know about her? What has the author led you to feel about her?
4 Why do you think the author has repeated the phrase 'or as good as' at the end of two paragraphs?
5 Why do you think the author has included a snatch of nursery rhyme?

Blurred boundaries

We have looked at the generally recognized subcategories of crime – though there are many others – but the distinctions between them are not absolute. Boundaries between them are frequently blurred. Many novels and television programmes that you may know probably will not fit exactly into any box. Is *Midsomer Murders* 'cosy crime' or police procedural?

How to decide what kind of crime novel to write

The analysis in this chapter should help you decide and show you which are the best commercial choices at the present time. If you are unfamiliar with any of the subgenres, I suggest you try reading one or two examples to get a taste. You never know, it might appeal to you.

However, the most important thing is this:

Focus point

You can only successfully write the kind of book you like to read.

To help you clarify your thoughts, try the following questionnaire.

Snapshot exercise

Think about the crime novels that you like to read. Which of these elements do you look for and enjoy?

1. a Fast-moving action
   b Trying to guess the murderer before the end
   c Getting to know the character of the sleuth
2. a Being carried along swiftly by the narrative
   b Being surprised by the solution
   c Being persuaded that this could actually have happened recently in real-life
3. a Snappy dialogue.
   b Trying to spot red herrings and unobtrusive clues.
   c Trying to spot when people are lying for some reason.
4. a Grim inner-city settings
   b Countryside or middle-class settings
   c Working-class settings

And, finally, which of these things annoy you most?

5. a Deliberately contrived cleverness of the plot
   b Gratuitous violence
   c One-dimensional characters

Rate yourself

Mostly 'a's – consider tackling 'realistic' crime, or the crime thriller mode.

Mostly 'b's – classic detective, locked room mysteries or 'cosies' might appeal.

Mostly 'c's – take a look at police procedurals.

So, before we move on, let's take another look at the list of motives that you created earlier. (You did do that, didn't you? If not, put this book down and go and do it now.)

Edit exercise

1 Refine your 'motives' list. Has any of this chapter suggested motives that you hadn't thought about?

2 Choose three of the motives that most appeal to you. Who, in each case, is going to murder whom? Don't stick with the obvious, try out the possible alternatives, not forgetting the more unlikely ones. In our practice example, for instance, perhaps Henry murders Fred? Or Jo? Or both? What might make either Fred or Jo decide to murder *him*?

3 Try out alternative times, genders, races and/or places. For example, is Jo male or female? Is this central New York and a gang scene? Or a peaceful village in deepest Somerset? Or a different time and place entirely where they are all slaves on a plantation? Can you see how any of these changes might dictate other things – the method of murder, for example?

Sometimes the most interesting plot derives from the least obvious possibilities.

Crime gives you lots of scope. Don't try combining it with more fantastic genres.

Linda Bennett, Crime editor, Salt Publishing

'Don't mix genres... It's very annoying to read a perfectly competent murder story almost to the end, and suddenly be confronted with a dénouement that claims that the perpetrator was a witch, or a time traveller who has since gone off to the eighteenth century!'

Where to next?

Your Edit exercise should have helped you see how the setting of the book is a vital element. In Chapter 2 we shall look at creating settings – both in time and place – and how to make them vivid for your reader.

2

Creating settings

We saw in the last chapter how important setting is, to the extent of actually defining some subgenres. It can even suggest which murder method is available. (A pitchfork is an unlikely weapon in an inner-city slum, though it might therefore be a peculiarly interesting one!)

The setting of the story – both in time and place – determines the society and culture in which your characters will move. It affects not only the kinds of lives they live but the whole social attitude to crime, justice and retribution that applies. (If you can't immediately see the force of this, imagine someone who puts an unwanted baby out to die of cold and starvation, choosing a place where the corpse is likely to be eaten by dogs. A shocking criminal offence? In ancient Rome it was quite usual if a father doubted the child's paternity, suspected that it was not physically or mentally perfect – or simply did not want another girl. Perfectly legal, too.)

G.J. Demko

'There is [a] most important dimension of the genre that is too often ignored by readers and not fully appreciated by writers, and that is the setting or the geography over which the hero and villain and red herrings traipse. Its importance is unique to the genre and all too often taken for granted by the reader. The physical setting, type of legal system, types of people involved, the accessibility of the place of the crime, and many other characteristics are critical to the story.'

 Focus point

Setting is not simply the physical description of a scene. It is the whole context and ethos in which the crime occurs.

Why any setting must be established fast

Since the cultural setting is essential to the plot, readers need to get the context clear at once. They generally assume what they're familiar with. Thus, UK readers might assume it's modern Britain, and probably urban modern Britain, unless told otherwise. So if that is not the setting that you have in mind, it's essential to make that clear as soon as possible. It is disconcerting to have to change the mental picture part way through.

 Key idea

Unless the reader is told otherwise, the default position is to mentally place the story in the time and place in which they live themselves.

There are several techniques for indicating quickly that the book is not set in the here and now.

- **Preface the first chapter with the date or place, or both.** This is a bold approach, most suitable for distant times and civilizations very different from our own. Peter James and Lindsey Davis, to name but two, make constant use of it. (The latter's *Silver Pigs,* for instance, opens by placing us uncompromisingly in 'Rome: autumn–summer 70 AD').

- **Mention a place-name in the opening paragraph.** This may be in the action:

  Ralph walked down the Ramblas thoughtfully. How lively Barcelona always looked in spring.

  or in dialogue:

  'Mr Esmeeth?' the girl at the reception desk glanced at his reservation and handed him a key.

  'Welcome to Barthelona, Mr Esmeeth.' He'd thought that 'Smith' was innocuous enough, but she managed to make it sound memorable and odd.

- **Do the same thing with a date or season.**

  London was shaking off the winter of 1860 by degrees. Grey buds on grimy lime trees were attempting to emerge...

  Or use a defining historical event or personality

  A tattered election poster fluttered from a wall. 'Vote Atlee'.

- **Evoke the setting subtly, by drip-feeding hints.** This is the most effective method, but requires care. Ensure that there is some tell-tale detail very early on – anything from a piece of clothing or an implement, up to a full-scale historical event (watching a public execution, for instance), which warns the reader to get the mental picture right. But get your clues in early. In the first paragraph, if you can manage it.

Write now

Write an opening paragraph of at least 100 words, describing a setting that you think could be suitable for each of the following genres (these are outlined in the first chapter, if you skipped over it):

a   a 'cosy' crime

b   a Brit grit or noir story

c   a police procedural

d   a howdunnit novel.

Begin each paragraph with the words 'There was a body slumped against the wall.' Don't fidget with your first attempts; just write whatever comes. There will be an opportunity to revisit it again later in the chapter, when we've looked at some techniques.

Describing physical locations vividly

Do you remember when you were at school, being told to use all your senses when describing things? To make sure that you didn't just use visual imagery, but to think about sounds, smell and touch as well? It turns out that the teachers who urged this were 'righter than they knew' – though their advice was rather oversimplified and does not cover everything a crime writer needs to know.

What follows here is rather technical, but please bear with me and try to follow it. Many of my students – especially those who found a publisher – later told me that this was the single most important insight that they gained. But before we start, try out this little exercise. You'll see the point of it (I hope!) a little later on.

Snapshot exercise – part A

Set a timer (your mobile phone will do) and give yourself two minutes for the first part of this task. Then shut your eyes and try to remember your first day at school. (It is important that you shut your eyes, so the things that you can see don't prod your memory or distract you from the task in hand.) If you can't remember the first day, don't agonize, just try to remember the earliest time you can. When the two minutes are over, open your eyes and write down as much as possible of what you could recall.

What has that to do with writing crime? Well, recent experiments with brain-imaging have shown conclusively:

- that there are different cortices (or areas of the brain) that are devoted to different aspects of our experience. For our purposes, they can be broadly divided into four: dealing with visual information (what we see), audial (what we hear), kinaesthetic (what we feel – emotion, touch and atmosphere), and purely intellectual constructs (such as comparisons we make, conclusions we draw and our perceptions as to measurement). For our purposes, smell and taste will be included in the kinaesthetic group (though in fact they're slightly separate) as we don't have a large vocabulary for identifying them. However, perhaps because they're actually distinct, either can form a very potent kind of prompt.

- that memory is laid down simultaneously in all four cortices. (As you may know, stimulating one specific neuron of the brain will reliably produce a specific memory. That's why the smell of gym shoes may take us back to school-day changing rooms.)
- that all of us, unless we are physically or mentally impaired, can access all these cortices at will, BUT
- that when trying to recall a memory different individuals use different ones for preference, and always search these first, AND (most importantly for us)
- that memory and imagination register activity in exactly the same parts of the brain. We use recalled experience in order to imagine something new.

So what does this mean for the writer? One essential thing. Your readers' imaginations may work differently from yours. In fact, this is statistically the case for one in four of them. So if you create a striking visual picture of a scene, but your reader responds primarily to audial or kinaesthetic cues, your clever evocation may not strike a chord. Or vice versa, of course. Yet all the strands are available to you. All you have to do is to work out what your own preferred ones are and deliberately add the others – a visual detail, a sound, a smell, a simile or fact – so that all your readers will be catered for.

Focus point

Your readers' imaginations may work differently from yours. Make sure that you help them to imagine the scene you have in mind.

Snapshot exercise – part B

Look back at your scribblings about your first memories of school.

1 Are they full of visual images? Colours? Pictures? Objects? Light? People's hairstyles and the things they wore?

2 Was sound important in your memory? Did you recall a teacher's voice, a song, the sound of children playing, what someone said to you?

3 Or was your memory chiefly what you felt? Your emotions? Feeling proud, or overwhelmed? Or was it full of movement?

Games you played? Walking in the classroom? The touch of someone's hand? The feel of something, or perhaps a smell?

4 Or were you more concerned with how the desks were placed, how many children there were, how big the classroom was? Did you make mental comparisons – the chair was bigger or smaller than at home? Were there any numbers at all in what you wrote, or any mention of height, or length or width? Did you remember the subject of pictures of the wall?

Go through and mark each memory with the number of the paragraph to which you think it most relates. Do you have mostly 1, 2, 3 or 4? (Many crime writers score quite heavily in either 2 or 4. The 'construct' thinker is usually the one that's most at home with puzzles.) Was there any classification that did not occur at all? What does this tell you about what you need to add to make your descriptions really come to life? (If you still doubt this, try this recall exercise on a group of friends – the results may surprise you!)

Key idea

Pay particular attention to including the kinds of cue (visual, audial, etc.) that you don't tend to use yourself.

When a sketch map may be a useful tool

A final word on getting settings right. People who have a strongly visual or intellectual imagination will keep a mental map of the setting you create. They will notice if the door, which opened on to the passage on page one, suddenly leads into the front room half-way through. If you do not have a vivid picture of the geography, draw yourself a little map – perhaps even sketching where the furniture is placed, if that is mentioned in the narrative. Do the same with streets, or country lanes. It doesn't have to be elaborate. Just make sure that your landmarks remain in the same place, and your characters could reach them in the timeframe you suggest. You will save yourself a lot of time and trouble later on. If you have a different kind of memory, you won't need this at all.

Are you the kind of thinker who would benefit from a sketch map of the setting that you choose? Try this little exercise.

Take yourself back into school again. Do you have a clear picture of where the classroom lay? Can you imagine walking out of it and knowing what you'd find outside the door? Try drawing a little sketch map as you picture it, and see if it helps you work out where things were. If you find this difficult, you probably need to make one while you're writing crime.

Edit exercise

Look again at one of the opening paragraphs you wrote in the 'Write now' exercise earlier in the chapter. Is it purely visual? Or almost all intellectual – what the building was used for and where it stood in relation to the road? Is there any sound or smell in your scene at all? When you think about it, would there be any? What elements – sound, smell, factual detail or visual element – could you add to make your mini setting come more vividly to life? Try rewriting it, including some of these.

Why adjectives can be your ally or your enemy

Perhaps you can now also see why new writers are advised not to use too many adjectives (pure describing words), especially in the opening paragraphs. What is really meant here is that too much visual description will 'switch' some readers off, for the reasons we've been looking at. This does not mean that you can't describe things, quite the opposite – but look for other ways of doing it.

If you want to say 'the wall was very big', rephrase it in a way that uses other senses than the visual. This isn't hard to do. Say 'it was higher than the spreading fir tree next to it' and the comparison has already invited the reader to use the 'construct' mode of thought. Say 'it was so high that he could not see over it, even when he was standing on tiptoe' and you've invoked a kinaesthetic image. (Can you see that you've been invited, now, to imagine first a tree and then someone on tiptoe? Yet this is still a 'description' of the wall.)

This is not only to assist those who are not naturally visual. By involving more channels in the reader's brain, you make everybody imagine your scene more vividly. Including you! And it is not 'cheating' – lots of authors go back afterwards and revise a scene by systematically adding more vivid details of this kind. Some rely on instinct; others have the benefit of knowing why it works!

With all this in mind:

- **Cut down your adjectives,** especially those not working for their keep. Describing a 'grey' granite building is really saying nothing at all. Granite buildings are usually 'grey'. A 'tall granite building' is a little better (though not much): the reader will assume that you mean 'tall' in relation to other buildings. A 'windowless' building, on the other hand, is quite evocative – one expects a building to have windows, so the adjective is doing something here.

Mark Twain

'When you catch an adjective, kill it. No, I don't mean utterly, but kill most of them – then the rest will be valuable. They weaken when they are close together. They give strength when they are wide apart.'

- **Don't use too many adjectives at once:** 'A tall, windowless, graffiti-covered granite building' is too much information at one time. Try limiting yourself to one or two at any point. Start with just the really vital ones, then add the others in later paragraphs or infiltrate them as you go along. You'll find this a useful ploy in any case. By adding further details and adjectives right throughout the text you keep the setting fresh. If you just describe it once, and let it go at that, the reader will gradually forget about it too.

Key idea

When writing a description, limit the adjectives that you apply to any one thing at any one time – spread them over several sentences, paragraphs or scenes.

- **Shorten your sentences:** One might think that a descriptive sentence like this, 'It was a windowless building with peeling paint and a graffiti-covered door that dangled from one hinge' would be ideal. In fact, if you cut this description into two, you will double its effectiveness. 'It was a windowless building with peeling paint. A graffiti-covered door was dangling from one hinge.' Now, you will see, the description of our 'building' has moved on and the second sentence is (apparently) describing something else – the door (which is actually a detail of the 'building').

Snapshot exercise

Look at those two sentences again. Can you find a way to do the same again – divide each image into two, in each case describing something new? Feel free to add some details of your own – the subject of the graffiti, the colour of the paint. Can you 'feel' how this brings the description into sharper focus? Try out variations. Which version do you prefer?

- Better still, you can evoke a place by having someone in it. The reader's attention is generally more drawn to people than to places, so by describing what the character is doing you can evoke the scene quite vividly.

Workshop exercise

Look at the following opening paragraphs by a master of the craft:

Brain tissue clung like wet, grey lint to the sleeves of Dr Kay Scarpetta's surgical gown, and the front of it was splashed with blood. Stryker saws whined, running water drummed and bone dust sifted through the air like flour. Three tables were full. More bodies were on the way. It was Tuesday, January 1, New Year's Day.

She didn't need to rush toxicology to know her patient had been drinking before he pulled the shotgun's trigger with his toe. The instant she'd opened him up, she detected the putrid pungent smell of booze as it breaks down in the body...

Patricia Cornwell, *Scarpetta*

Ask yourself: where are we? How do you know? What
visual clues are there? What audial ones? Any kinaesthetic?
Any intellectual ones (comparisons, accurate figures,
measurements, logical conclusions)? How many actual
adjectives are there? How many at a time?

How vivid and memorable is the scene? (By the way, what is
a 'stryker saw'? Do you know? What do you think it is?) What
kind of novel is this going to be?

Of course, there will be more than one location in your book, and
you will have to evoke each one of them in turn. But the techniques
here apply to all of them – not just to the opening paragraphs.
And that is logical. Your setting is, after all, the whole culminative
context of your imaginary world.

How to write enough description and avoid too much

You will have noticed, being a crime reader and alert to clues, that
in the previous Snapshot exercise, there was a reference to bringing
the scene into 'sharp focus'. Generally, of course, that is a splendid
thing. If you are writing realistic crime, then 'sharp focus' is exactly
what you want: short brutal sentences and changes of attack, with
very little descriptive embroidery. If you are writing 'cosies', this
may not be true. Think photography. Longer sentences and slightly
more frequent adjectives are the equivalent of the 'soft focus' setting
on the camera. There won't be graffiti, peeling paint and broken
doors – unless we're in a barn that's not been used for years. Go
instead for soft colour adjectives, plenty of kinaesthetic detail (a
chilly wind or grasses clutching someone's ankles as they walk).
However, this is not an excuse to let your adjectives go wild, or any
other descriptive detail. Readers will simply skip the passage if you
do. Think of 'cosy description' as a careful selection of evocation
cues for 'soft-focus' purposes.

Edit exercise

Look again at the opening of the 'cosy crime' you wrote in the
'Write now' exercise earlier in the chapter. What is the mood of it?
Are there any ways in which you think you might improve it now?
Think for yourself what scents and sounds there are. Is there

an abstract fact or logical comparison that you can add – one specific flower name would be enough, provided that is not just a cliché like 'a rose' ('a tea-rose' is altogether different). Remember that the season is important here. Your setting is not merely a physical place.

Think back to the Patricia Cornwell extract. How much have you managed to tell your readers in roughly the same space?

When a little too much is exactly what you need

Too many adjectives – and too much detailed description generally – are inclined to lull the reader. Sometimes he or she simply skips it, as we've said before. Obviously you don't want this, as a general rule – especially on page one, or your reader will simply put the book back on the shelf. However, we are talking about crime, where ordinary writing rules don't always operate. Sometimes that 'switch-off' mechanism is what you're aiming for.

Key idea

If you want to hide a clue, put it in a longish paragraph of descriptive detail about three-quarters down.

Provided that doesn't seem wholly out of place, the reader will probably glide over it – thanks to the 'lulling function' of sustained descriptive prose. So if you want to hide a poker, keep it in full sight. Give a glowing description of the living room and add an adjective to everything else: mention the fresh flowers, the ornate mantle-clock, the artfully posed coal bucket and poker on the hearth, and the expensive Turkish rugs beside the fire. The chances are your reader will hardly notice the poker. The flurry of adjectives will lull them into glossing over it. However, be careful where you place your 'clue'. Too early in the list, and it will draw the eye – too late and it will linger in the subconscious memory. (It seems the average reader 'touches down' to register the last-named item in a list, in which case you should try to make that something notable, so that attention is further drawn from your casually mentioned weapon.)

So 'too much' description all at once is sometimes a technique. That is the *only* excuse for writing it. But it's a useful thing to know. Once you have realized that you're deliberately triggering the reader to 'switch off', it should convince you to avoid such passages elsewhere. Now you've identified this trick of hiding clues, it may spoil your enjoyment of some classic crime novels, but you can have your fun by spotting where it's used, instead!

How to set a scene in just a line or two

If you're not using many adjectives but creating a vivid setting is an imperative, what strategies remain?

- **Describing a place by drawing attention to objects in the scene** – concentrating on the ones that paint the mood (like the graffiti or the brain tissue, above). You can even add an adjective here and there, as long as each one is describing something different. However – as with the adjectives themselves – limit the number of objects and don't use them all at once. Five or six is generally enough, or your prose will be in danger of reading like a list. Save a few items to feed into the story later on, to keep the reader actively thinking about the setting.
- **Putting people in the scene** – as in the Scarpetta extract – though notice, in that passage, the character is still surrounded by a whirlpool of activity. We know what she is thinking and what she has just done, but as we first meet her – and her environment – she does not actually move. (Look back for a moment, if you are in doubt.) This is striking, and many authors use some version of this technique.
- **Adding action to the scene.** This action can be violent, but it does not have to be. It does not even have to be a human doing it. Peter James begins *Sweet Heart* with 'The dog scampered under the rotting gate.' Movement plunges the reader straight into the plot, and makes them ask questions straight away. (What is this place and who owns the dog?) Yet it still suggests location, to some extent at least. (We are clearly out of doors – though until we read on that is all we know. But did you imagine some semi-urban scene with a road and fence as well? Remember the default position?)
- **Using dialogue,** which is also action of a kind (we will come back to this) and is sometimes a quick way of sketching in a place. Where do you think we are, in the following text?

'Your usual, guv'ner?' the spotty youth behind the bar reached out a grimy, tattooed hand towards the pump marked 'Millar's Mild'.

Focus point

Action, things and people can indicate a place better than a string of adjectives.

Time, as well as place, is part of every setting you create

Historical crime is a subgenre in itself, but time is just as much a part of any setting as the place, and the two are inextricably linked – since of course the same place may be quite different at different periods.

- This can be a specific time and place, for example New York, New Year's Eve, 1923, or a more generic one such as a small village in the 1980s – and the choice you make for how specific the setting is will have big implications for the book.

- Picking 'closed world' settings, in time as well as place, can be a great device for murder mysteries. Take, for example, Christie's *Murder on the Orient Express*: the perpetrator has to be someone on the train, and the journey gives a finite time in which we know the crime must have occurred.

- A time constraint can also be key in shaping and adding tension to a narrative. (For instance, if your sleuth can't solve the crime within a certain time, they will have to let everyone go, or, in a crime thriller, at midnight the kidnapped victim will be shot).

Write now

Look at the opening paragraphs about the body by the wall in the earlier 'Write now' exercise. What elements would be different if the scene was set 100 years ago? Two hundred? A thousand? In Anglo-Saxon times? In New York on New Year's Eve 1923?

Choose one of those times and rework the paragraph – or do the same with a period that you have chosen yourself. Then carry on the scene a little. Write about a page.

Do you feel that choosing a different time setting would suit your writing style and interests?

Key idea

Setting is about time as well as place.

Settings suggest people

Settings suggest people – so much so that tension can emerge from putting characters into places where they don't 'belong'. 'Realistic' crime is often set in dingy modern streets while 'cosies' have a village or rural atmosphere. Obviously the types of people living in each place will be different. This is not type-casting, as some people suppose – environment really is a significant part of how people speak, act, dress and think.

Orison Swett Marden

'Your outlook upon life, your estimate of yourself, your estimate of your value are largely colored by your environment. Your whole career will be modified, shaped, molded by your surroundings, by the character of the people with whom you come in contact every day.'

This is not to say that all characters in one setting will come out of one mould, but the kind of place they live in will affect them all – though perhaps in different ways – and it is essential for an author to be aware of this. Who is lying dead on the dingy garage workshop floor? Whose body is sprawled on the expensive Turkish rug in a Madrid penthouse flat?

Conversely, putting a character into a scene in which they do not fit creates an immediate feeling of interest and unease. We all know what it's like to feel slightly out of place and capturing this feeling can add tension to the plot. A nun in a casino is a startling idea, just as a croupier in a nunnery would be – or a comfy country matron in a jet-set city club: part of the interest is what they are doing there.

Snapshot exercise

Choose two of the opening paragraphs which you wrote earlier. Spend a few minutes getting a fuller picture of the corpse beside the wall, making a quick note in each case of whatever you thought first: how old? In what clothing (if any)? Of what race? Is there any evidence of the cause of death? Now deliberately rethink – making the body someone who does not 'fit' the scene. Does that make a difference? What questions does it raise?

Where to next?

So, we've looked at settings. Let's move on now to the people who emerge from them. In Chapter 3 we shall look at techniques for creating lively characters, the different levels of development required (depending on people's importance to the plot), and how and where crime writing may differ from other genres in this.

3

Creating characters

The role of character is just as important in crime fiction as it is in other genres – indeed, it might be argued to be more important since relationships and motivation play such a key role. As in other fiction, there is an important distinction to be made between major, minor and walk-on characters and it is crucial, too, to have characters reveal their personality through actions, speech and (where possible) thoughts rather than for the reader to be given a pen-portrait by the author. Also in this chapter, we will begin to look at point of view – the mindset through which the story is filtered as it unfolds.

Jack Hart

'A novel rises or falls on the strength of its characters.'

Why crime novels depend on character

- Crime novels depend on motives – human emotions and weaknesses – and your characters are the ones that have them. Every person in your story will have different feelings, drives and traits, and to each individual those are the important ones.
- Unlike other genres, mystery crime characters don't develop very much; they merely reveal the kind of person that they are (with the possible exception of the sleuth). Since you don't want your reader to know from the outset who the killer, is you will need to make everybody's inner lives and emotions clear, at least apparently, though obviously for the killer not all will be revealed.
- Don't neglect your criminal. Even the villain is the centre of their own story as they see it and believes that what they do is in some way justified. This is especially true of thrillers. A deranged killer with no moral sense killing at random may be interesting news, but does not make good fiction because we cannot empathize. There may be a story about how police catch up with the killer, but even that depends on the motives and emotions of those involved.

Why it is important to have 'enough' different characters

Key idea

In 'puzzle' crime one needs a range of characters in order for there to be a mystery at all.

Even in thrillers it is rarely viable to have only two characters, as can sometimes happen in other genres. But every extra character must have a proper role, which many be any or all of the following:

- as background or professional back-up for the sleuth (the sidekick)
- to create professional tension or problems for the sleuth (their boss or enemies)
- to create a background for the victim (usually as friends, colleagues, employees or family)
- to give witness accounts (which may vary subtly) of actions and events – enabling the author to distribute clues (apparently random bystanders, employees, etc.)
- to do the same for personalities, allowing the sleuth (and reader) to build up a picture of the cast. (This is an extremely important role, which we shall look at in more detail later on, but can be fulfilled by any character.)
- to provide a variety of motives for the crime (in whodunnits of all kinds usually either several characters have potential motives, or nobody appears to have one. Even in the latter case, a range of people who don't have motives is an essential tool.)
- to take part in deliberate 'red herring' happenings which serve to divert the reader from the truth.

Snapshot exercise

Go back to your corpse beside the wall from Chapter 2. (If you are not working through these chapters in order, try to get a mental picture of a body now. It should be lying by a wall – any type of person, any type of wall – but try to make your picture as specific as you can and capture that in a short paragraph before continuing with this exercise.) If you have not already decided on a cause of death, do so now.

List the relationships that this dead person might have had. Then ask yourself, what kind of motives could each of those people have had to murder him/her? You should have a list of motives made in Chapter 1 but, if you've skipped that, try the seven deadly sins. Don't try to invent whole characters just yet; simply note how these people are connected to the corpse and you've created a list of suspects for the crime. (Note that you start with the character to find the motives – writing plots the other way about tends to produce more 'cardboard exemplars' than vibrant individuals.)

The difference between major, minor and walk-on characters

Crime novels can differ from other genres in the differences between major, minor and walk-on characters. Many writing tutorials advise that you should:

- decide at the outset who are the 'major characters', whose 'story' this actually is
- have two such characters at most and work to make them fully rounded personalities
- make it clear to the reader from the outset who they are
- keep them central to the storyline throughout
- ensure that anything else (including subplots) is peripheral – though probably in some way relevant – to them
- differentiate between them and 'minor characters' – that is people who surround them, but whose personalities do not have to be so rounded as readers do not need to understand as much about the way they act and think.

CRIME MYSTERY NOVELS

Crime mystery novels – whodunnits, howdunnits and even whydunnits – simply do not work in this way. For one thing 'major characters' are not always what they seem. Usually, there are the following:

- **Overtly major characters,** for whom the advice, above, applies. The most obvious is the sleuth, of course, and the story may be seen in terms of their attempt to find the killer and solve the mystery. However, the other clearly 'central' character – the corpse, on whom the whole plot ultimately depends – is no longer in a position to do anything at all, so we can only learn about that character through what other people say and do. (Even if the victim is alive at the beginning of the narrative, we rarely get a chance to get a full look at their lives and really understand them before the killer strikes – otherwise, of course there would be no mystery.)
- A 'hidden' major character – that is, the murderer. The author knows who that is, but the sleuth and reader don't – and obviously mustn't until the denouement. So the usual strictures about major characters constantly being in the reader's consciousness absolutely do not follow here. If you did that with your murderer, you'd give the game away. Yet the reader must understand this 'hidden' character as well as any other

major character – motives, methods, weaknesses and thought processes – or think they do. How can that be managed?

The trick is to make lots of characters potentially major ones, which means that you have to tell, or preferably show, the reader more about each one than you'd expect in another sort of book. (Too many full-blown characters might sink a light romance, but here your reader knows that any of the cast you introduce may be the murderer.) On the other hand, there is an optimum. One or two potential suspects aren't usually enough, but a reader can't really hold many more than five or six of them in mind. Which brings us to the so-called 'minor' characters.

- **Minor characters** are the ones that in other kinds of book have subsidiary roles, often to act as confidant. The sidekick to the sleuth is often genuinely one of these, and other people – neighbours, casual friends and workmates of the victim, or people connected to the suspects in some way – may also appear to occupy that sort of role. However, in a mystery crime, any of these (except the sidekick, as a rule) may turn out to be the killer in the end – they are simply artfully disguised as somebody peripheral.

Note that where such a 'minor' character' in fact commits the crime, we must meet them early in the book. Little details can then be given from the start, which later turn out to be significant. (Don't cheat by springing something without 'seeding' clues and information in this way – you want the reader to think 'Why didn't I realize that?' rather than 'I don't know enough about that character to understand their motives.') But since your 'hidden' killer must not be conspicuous, it follows that other minor characters – like the major ones – still need to be more fully drawn than they would be elsewhere.

> ## Key idea
>
> In a murder mystery the distinction between major and minor characters may be deliberately blurred.

- **'Walk-on' characters** are different. They are people who are needed in the story for the role they occupy, but whose personalities are not significant: very often they are simply there because of what they do – taxi drivers, waiters, hotel receptionists. A quick test is to ask yourself: would any other person performing that same job do just as well? If that is the case, then you have a 'walk-on character'. Don't waste time with building up a character for them. Generally, they don't require a name. If they come back later in the narrative, then give them one strong, visual attribute – the taxi-driver with a snake tattoo, the hotel receptionist with ginger hair – and let it go at that. If we meet them again, we will remember them. These are what Janet Burroway unkindly calls 'flat characters', because they don't need to be fully rounded. But don't be tempted to simply sketch a generic nobody; there must be something about everyone we meet that is distinct and memorable.

Ford Madox Ford

'If you're going to have a character appear in a story long enough to sell a newspaper, he'd better be real enough that you can smell his breath.'

CRIME THRILLERS

With these the more usual advice applies. We are not looking for a suspect here: the reader usually knows who that is – or at least that there is one – from the start, and the victim is (generally) still alive but under threat. There may or may not be a 'rescuer', trying to circumvent the threat. These are your 'major characters' and must be as fully realized as possible. Indeed, we often need to get inside their heads, so that the reader can fully understand the 'threat', empathize with the intended victim, and be aware of how dangerous, focused and peculiar the would-be assassin (or whatever) is.

You may need 'minor characters' who are friends, associates, confidants and generally people to whom the victim turns, and these can indeed be less developed than your major ones – though be sure that they continue to be individuals, not merely stereotypes. Ensure that each exhibits a distinct personality, by contrast with the 'walk-on' characters, who still function exactly as above – with one notable exception.

It has been noted that people will pick up the morning mail while declaring with conviction to the police officer that nobody has called. Thrillers can use that to effect. For example, your victim/ heroine has locked herself into her house, having received a phone threat from the would-be murderer. Then she sees a post office van pull up outside. What a relief! She's friendly with the postman … who, of course, is not a walk-on character at all.

How much you need to know about your characters, and why that is not the same as what the reader needs to know

It is often urged that the reader needs a complete picture of all major characters:

- In a crime thriller, this is largely true. However, tread with care. As with over-writing descriptions of a place, too much trivial information can switch a reader off. What the reader needs is enough insight to make the characters come strongly from the page.

- In a crime mystery, even this does not apply. For one thing there are more potential 'major' characters and, for another, if the reader really had 'a complete picture' of all the characters, there would be no plot. The trick is to make them feel as if they do.

But though you won't tell your reader everything, *you* should know as much about your major characters as if they were your friends or personal enemies.

So how is this achieved? Lots of books suggest exercises about creating or exploring characters by mentally filling in a questionnaire, as in the Snapshot exercise below.

Snapshot exercise

Try the following questionnaire and use it to create a character who might walk into one of the scenes that you created earlier.

Age?

Sex?

Name?

Profession/occupation, if any?

Place of work, if any?

Usual method of transport?

Education?

Usual clothes?

Lives where?

With whom (if anyone?)

Significant others (including friends, pets and family)?

Preferred leisure activity?

Most treasured possession?

Major strengths?

Weaknesses?

This kind of exercise is not a bad idea. You should be able to do something similar for all your major and even minor characters – but only after you have created them. Don't start with it, however, except for the purposes of this exercise. It makes for mechanical thinking. It is tempting to think up random answers and then try to imagine someone who fits with what you've said, supposing that 'creates a character'. It doesn't. It's the other way about. You'll know these things about your fictional characters *after* you've got them in your head – had them grow out of your scene and watched them act and speak. Not that you'll tell the reader all of it, of course. As a rule of thumb, use no more than three-quarters of what you know yourself.

Snapshot exercise

Repeat the questionnaire above, but this time apply it to a friend. Can you see the difference? Now you are searching for information that you either know, or at least can make a guess about, based on what you already know about their character and life – which is exactly what you should be doing with your imaginary characters.

You want to build someone with motives and personality, not someone who wears purple underwear.

In the same way, some tutors advocate cutting random pictures out of magazines and creating a biography to fit the photograph. My own view, again, is that this is back to front. Once you have a mental image of a character, it may be very helpful to glance through supplements and try to find someone who resembles that – in the same way as you might be struck by a magazine photograph that looks rather like a friend. On the other hand, the model in the picture presumably does not arise from the background and life circumstances that you are imagining – and we have already stressed that this impacts on almost everything: posture, dress, self-presentation and even facial expression. Have the courage of your own imagination and let your people rise up from the backgrounds that they have.

Why the characters that you create should not be representations of people that you know

Don't just describe your granny or anyone else you know – and for much the same reasons as not using photographs:

- Your granny is/was the product of her own time, upbringing and circumstances and if you are writing fiction your characters are products of quite different ones.
- You are writing about people, some of whom are murderers or potential murderers. If that does not describe your granny and her friends, leave her out of it.
- Writers are often advised to 'write about what they know'. Unless you know a lot of killers, kidnappers, rapists and the like, that won't apply to you – especially in the creation of your characters. (If you are a police officer, don't do it anyway, at least in fiction; otherwise, as you'll realize, you might find yourself in court!) Have confidence in creating people from within your mind – although, of course, they may, and should, have traits you recognize.

Why good characters must have substantial flaws and even killers some redeeming quality

Stephen King

'*Bad writing usually arises from a stubborn refusal to tell stories about what people actually do, to face the fact, let us say, that murderers sometimes help old ladies cross the street.*'

If you want to make your characters as real as possible, remember that almost no one is wholly evil. Some 'humanizing' feature in your murderer will make a better plot and – conversely – may even make a villain still more sinister. (Remember Blofeld's cat in the James Bond movie?) Also, remember that even killers generally believe that they are justified. If we don't understand this, we don't understand the crime.

John Rogers

'You don't really understand an antagonist until you understand why he's a protagonist in his version of the world.'

Neither is any normal human (including your detective) wholly good – even if they are female, black, disabled or otherwise politically correct. Giving them human frailties will make them more sympathetic to the reader, not less. It is hard to empathize with people with no faults. This is why 'character-creating' questionnaires almost always suggest you think of one to introduce. But selecting a random 'frailty' is not enough – it must grow out of the personality that you've created, and conform with it.

Write now

You should have a fairly clear picture of your corpse by now, so write a couple of connected paragraphs about their character. (Remember that you need to know such details as the name, even if your readers will not know it yet.) Make your piece biographical as well as descriptive (try applying some of the questions from the questionnaire) and including, if you can, the attitudes, failings, past deeds, secrets – or even attributes – which might have driven any or all of the people on your 'list of suspects' to commit this homicide.

Some sort of 'character sketch' like this about your corpse will serve you well when you begin to write, or edit, your own crime mystery – though your readers will never see it (in this form, certainly). However, it will help you to ensure that the character of your victim is a coherent one. If you propose to write crime thrillers, rather than mysteries, do this for your villain, so you know them thoroughly.

The role of physical description in a crime novel

Contrary to popular belief, physical description of characters is not always necessary, especially for major characters who are also narrators. (We shall return to this in detail when we look at viewpoint later in the chapter.) You will notice that what has been said about creating characters has been mostly about personality – their motives and the way they act and think – rather than about the way they look. However, we do make judgements about people in real life based on appearance – and especially what they wear – so it is helpful to offer a quick visual sketch of an incoming character.

Otherwise treat physical description of people as though it were the description of a place: keep it brief, don't use too many adjectives at once, and feed it bit by bit. But bear in mind that details of appearance can also sometimes be a clue, in which case the rules for hiding it apply. The exception is when a witness or a sleuth is describing somebody – but even there, try to break it up, perhaps with other lines of dialogue, so that it doesn't come out as a wodge of text.

We have already noted that a one-line description can be enough to identify a 'walk-on' character. However, there is one important point to bear in mind:

Key idea

When you do write physical description make sure that it remains consistent through the narrative. This is more important in crime than any other genre.

If Mrs Bloggs has blue eyes on page 1, but is mentioned as having green eyes on page 54, that is a *clue* – this isn't the same person, though it purports to be. It is not acceptable to do this by mistake. Keep a note or check back, if your visual picture isn't clear enough.

Key idea

Visual description is useful, but probably the least important part of creating rounded characters.

Focus point

When someone asks you what someone is 'like' they don't want a physical description, they want a description of character. That is what your readers want from you as well.

Snapshot exercise

Give yourself five minutes maximum. Write two sentences of physical description of your dotty spinster from the previous exercise who inherited the house, from the point of view of the police officer to whom she first reports finding the corpse.

How does this compare to your initial attempt at an opening paragraph?

What is meant by 'viewpoint' characters and how these are portrayed

A 'viewpoint character', as the name suggests, is the member of the cast from whose point of view we see the story at that point. This may be someone calling themselves 'I', or simply the person whose mental processes we are following at this point in the narrative. We shall return to this in greater detail later in the book.

While we are in the mindset of that character, it is perfectly reasonable not to describe their looks at all. Other people can do it, if the viewpoint changes later in the book. If the viewpoint character is the narrator throughout, you needn't dwell on visual appearance, unless it is important to the plot. Of course, you may offer the occasional clue, but avoid the cliché of people looking at their own reflections in mirrors, lakes and things as a way of describing how they look. Apart from name, age, sex, race and social standing – which you should make clear in conversation as soon as possible – the reader will be quite happy to create their own physical picture of the narrator.

When we know a person's thoughts, we understand their personality. If you want a sympathetic narrator, make them think charitable thoughts, especially about others. For example, 'She was obscenely fat, poor thing' rather than 'She was obscenely fat.' That will do more to make the reader think of the character as 'kind' than any amount of your telling them as much.

Unspoken thoughts are more telling than dialogue for this, because there are no social restraints. A character may declare a point of view, but what people say they think, and what they actually do think, can be quite different.

We believe what someone thinks, even over what we see them do or say. Someone who pays a compliment, while thinking quite the opposite, is hardly guilty of crime, but we won't be surprised to find that they are treacherous.

In crime thrillers (as distinct from mysteries) you may want to alternate between the viewpoint of the victim and of the person who is offering the threat. Physical description may have a strong place here: the 'villain' glories in the victim's looks, dwelling on fragility and prettiness, while their own appearance may not be disclosed until the end. Again, however, inward thoughts are the most effective way of showing character. Is your victim innocent, frail and panicking, or feisty and planning to knee the villain in the groin?

So, thoughts are the most effective way of showing character, but only with a viewpoint character. Anything we're told about the thoughts of other people in the cast is filtered through the author or someone who *is* a viewpoint character, so the illusion of 'uncensoredness' is lost.

Workshop exercise

Look at the following short extracts from the opening pages of two different crime novels:

A

Her name was Andrea Thomson. She wasn't a doctor – she'd made that clear at their first meeting. Nor was she a 'shrink' or 'therapist'. 'Career analysis' was what it had said on Rebus's daily sheet.

2:30 –3:15: Career analysis. Rm3.16

With Ms Thomson. Which had become Andrea at the moment of introduction. Which was yesterday. Tuesday. A 'get-to-know' session, she'd called it.

She was in her late thirties, short and large-hipped. Her hair was a thick mop of blond with some darker streaks showing through. Her teeth were slightly oversized. She was self-employed, didn't work for the police full-time.

'Do any of us?' Rebus had asked yesterday. She'd looked a bit puzzled.

Ian Rankin, *Resurrection Men*

B

Coppers: they like to catch you unawares. That's why they beat on your door at 6 o'clock in the morning.

I'd gone downstairs ready to give whoever it was a mouthful for waking the kids up, and opened the door to find two of them standing there. They weren't in uniform, but they have a look, a smell, and I knew what they were as soon as I saw them. I swallowed, my mouth suddenly dry.

'James Mitchell?' asked the hard-looking one in the leather jacket. I peered over his shoulder and saw a couple of patrol cars at the kerb.

I nodded. 'How can I help you?' I wondered what they'd found and where. Nobody would have talked. I was sure of that.

Julia Morrigan, *Barbed Wire*

Consider the techniques. Who is the 'viewpoint' character in each case? What do we know about their looks (if anything)? Their age? Their outlook? Their respective backgrounds and/or occupations? Is this information stated, or implied? Do we see the other people in the scene objectively, or only through the eyes of the viewpoint character? If the latter, does the description tell us anything about our informant's attitudes and personality?

Edit exercise

Look at any of the opening 'setting' paragraphs you wrote. Try reworking it, writing the same information, but this time from the point of view of a 'viewpoint character'. This can be one of the list of suspects you created earlier, or the sleuth, the sidekick or the murderer. Do not change any of the facts, but you should find that there is now a different view of things, and you may need to add details that were not there before. For instance, a friend or relative may react with shock and worry about the awkward way the corpse is lying. The sleuth will be looking out for clues – the murderer making sure that they haven't left any!

Why action and speech are essential to creating character

With viewpoint characters we have the benefit of thoughts, but there are other techniques for creating rounded character. It is best done not by author comment, but by what people say and do. You can create a rounded picture of a personality:

- through action
- through what other people think about the character
- through what other people say about the character
- by how other people react towards the character
- by how people alter when the character's not there
- by what the character says, particularly about others
- by how the character speaks and how people speak to them.

This is what is meant by disclosing, rather than describing, a character's personality.

- **Through action.** What your characters do – especially when alone – can strongly indicate the sort of person that they are. The reader will believe the evidence of deeds, much more than your description, every time. Don't say a character is 'cruel' – let the reader see them pulling legs off flies or mistreating their dog – preferably when no one else is watching. The same goes for almost any adjective you choose – vain, careless, proud – 'show us' don't tell us. Make your people act.

F. Scott Fitzgerald

'Action is character.'

- **Through what other people think about the character.** We can only trust the thoughts of viewpoint characters (as above), but if we see our police officer-narrator feeling pity for a murdered stripper, let's say, we are inclined to accept this judgement. We'll incidentally draw conclusions about the thinker, too – in either case.
- **Through what other people say about the character.** We've seen that an action is better than an adjective like 'cruel', but this won't work in every case, of course. If someone is 'beautiful', they can't show that by deeds. However, another character –

whether your viewpoint one or not – can comment on how beautiful they are. The reader will believe your characters, rather than your passages of descriptive prose. Again, this works best if the 'beautiful' character is not present at the time. It does not even have to be a compliment. 'Thinks that red hair and pretty face will get her anywhere!', for example. Or one character can describe another to someone who – like the reader – hasn't met them yet. This works well with witness statements. 'Dotty old biddy, but well-meaning in her way. Lives in a houseboat down by the canal.'

- **How other people react towards the character.** This is particularly useful for unpleasant characters, such as the spoiled daughter or the violent thug. For example, the mousy wife who's frightened to say boo and agrees with everything her husband says – even if she never says a word against him – makes it clear that he's a domineering type. If she declares that she keeps 'walking into doors', we may conclude that he is violent, too.
- **How people alter when the character's not there.** This is useful for creating suspicion. If the mousy wife seems much more confident when her husband's dead, we might begin to wonder where she was that night...
- **What the character says, particularly about others.** If they are always grumbling and finding fault, the reader will draw conclusions from this fact. If they are always spiteful behind their victims' backs, this will be noted, and remembered – much better than if you had to point it out explicitly.
- **How the character speaks – politely, rudely, humbly – and how people speak to them.** This is not only a matter of tone, but the type of language and grammar used. This is an essential element of dialogue, which we shall look at more fully in the next chapter.

Focus point

We learn about people from what they look like, but mostly from what they do, what people say about them and what they say themselves – and most of all what their self-image is, and how people behave around them.

Edit exercise

Look again at the biography that you created for the 'corpse'. In the light of this chapter, try recasting that from the point of view of:

a someone who loved him (mother, spouse, gay partner, daughter, son)

b someone who disliked him

c the murderer.

If interrogated by authority, which items in your biography would each one dwell on most? And why?

Focus point

In a crime novel 'truth' depends on the point of view of the character describing it.

Write now

Look back to the Edit exercise above. Write an 'interrogation' scene involving any one of the suggested characters. It doesn't have to be one of those you chose before. Make it a preliminary questioning conducted while looking for witness statements at the murder scene. Choose your own investigator, and limit yourself to one-third dialogue – remembering that actions, reactions and especially thoughts are what convey character. See whether you can create two distinct and interesting personalities, without directly describing either of them.

Aim for about 700 words.

Where to next?

We have already seen that internal thoughts and dialogue portray a character. In Chapter 4 we shall look more closely at the role of dialogue – what it is and how to write it realistically.

4

Writing dialogue

Dialogue can be tricky but, as we shall see in this chapter, it is a crucial part of the action in crime fiction. As in other fiction genres, it can be used, among other things, to reveal character, indicate relationships and to pass on crucial information. In a crime novel, it can also be also used to drop important clues in the development of the plot. In this chapter we will also explore register and some of the key ways in which a character's speech can be made individual and recognizable.

Janet Burroway

'The purpose (of dialogue) is never merely to convey information. Dialogue may do that, but it must also simultaneously advance the action or develop the characters.'

Key idea

Dialogue is not just conversation; it is part of the action.

Why dialogue is part of action

Dialogue appears to be a conversation between two (or more) of your fictional characters. This is an illusion. The dialogue is really part of the information that the writer is passing to the reader. It can be used for almost any purpose in this way. Here are a few examples:

- **To transmit facts directly:** one character tells another something factual, and the reader learns it, too. 'Gerry Benson, you must remember him – worked at the garage, till they caught him thieving sweets.'
- **To pass on information incidentally:** 'I wouldn't care to live in a great house like his.'
- **To convey the speaker's attitude,** which is not necessarily the same as the surface meaning of the words.'Gerry Benson? He's the blue-eyed boy round here. If there's a f**k-up you can bet he was a million miles away. Two-year trained is Gerry – you ask anyone.' How would you describe the speaker's attitude?
- **To describe another character** – their appearance or their personality, as we saw in the last chapter.This may be flattering, 'He's a really nice fellow – and good looking, too!' or otherwise, 'Whatever has Norah been doing with her hair? Call that a razor cut? Looks as if a chimpanzee's been gnawing it.'
- **To reveal the character of the speaker:** 'Well, Mr Benson, if you won't tell me what I want to know, perhaps you'd rather take a little walk with me? You see this knife? There are several interesting things that I can do with it – most of them rather painful, I'm afraid.'

- **To indicate action without spelling out events:** 'What are you doing? Put that gun down, Gerry! It isn't what you think! He's only...! Oh God, Gerry – what have you done?'

Elmore Leonard

'All the information you need can be given in dialogue.'

Snapshot exercise

Refer back to the extracts in the Workshop exercise in the previous chapter. There are three lines of explicit dialogue given there.

1 What facts, if any, do we learn from them?

2 What do we learn about the speakers' attitudes? To life in general? To other characters in the scene?

3 Do we learn anything about the speakers' characters?

Key idea

If an exchange does not add something to the plot, character or setting, it should not be there.

All this is standard advice to would-be novel writers of all kinds. However, this is crime, and – as usual – there are exceptions.

The special role of 'throwaways' in crime

Throwaways are tiny bits of dialogue that appear superfluous, but contain important clues intended to lead or mislead the reader. They may occur as:

- **seemingly trivial conversation,** containing a piece of information that is actually a clue, though you don't want your reader to recognize it yet. In which case, that item should not be the only piece of trivia in the exchange. So some of that piece of dialogue is – perforce – a kind of 'window-dressing', there to divert attention from the clue.

- **an apparently mundane utterance by a character,** which, if the reader has been following with care, indicates that the speaker is either lying, misled or misinformed. The remark may be disguised in a more rambling exchange, so that – again – it is not conspicuous.

These are, of course, related and deliberate techniques. Beware, however, of overusing them. 'Too much' chat – like 'too much' description – should be included carefully and only now and then, in the hope that the reader will glide over it. The idea – as everywhere – is to use minimum language to maximum effect.

Snapshot exercise

Read this piece of dialogue from a potential 'cosy' crime:

'There were a lot of people at the fete today,' Myra said, dropping a kiss on my bald spot as she put down her purchases. 'Saw that nice young estate agent and his wife, and that stuck-up couple from the butcher's shop. I thought I saw them talking to the vicar's wife, but she told me afterwards that they'd snubbed her, as well...'

This reads like simple chatter, but it could disguise a clue – and the average crime reader will be alert to this. So ask yourself the following:

- What significant information might be hidden here?
- Who might be lying?
- And who – by implication – wasn't at the fete?

So if a murder happened elsewhere while the fete was taking place, what possible suspects had the opportunity? Had it occurred to you, for instance, that the vicar wasn't mentioned? And what about the bald-headed narrator himself?

Every piece of dialogue you write should be susceptible to this kind of test.

How dialogue differs from connected prose

Firstly, it is set out differently. Dialogue is mostly rendered as exchanges of direct speech – the exact words spoken by each character in turn, enclosed in inverted commas ('like this'). This makes the page look 'lighter' and easier to read – so quick exchanges help to speed the narrative. It is a pretence at capturing the way that people speak. Another illusion!

Christopher Guest

'In real life, people fumble their words. They repeat themselves and stare blankly off into space and don't listen properly to what other people are saying. I find that kind of speech fascinating but (one should) never write dialogue like that because it doesn't look good on the page.'

On the other hand, it must read sufficiently like real conversation to be believable. This is where eavesdropping comes in. Listen to people speaking and – even if you don't want to be arrested for whipping out a notebook and recording what they say – try to remember the turns of phrase and note them afterwards. Pay attention to the structure, too. You will find that often it isn't completely grammatical; words will be missed out or contracted, and sentences will generally not be very long. Aim to make your dialogue like that, while still making the speeches earn their keep by 'advancing action, developing character' or disguising clues.

D. Wesley Smith

'Yeah, I know what your English Professor tried to tell you. But if your English Professor could make a living writing fiction, they would have been doing it.'

Register and its importance in writing dialogue

Focus point

Convincing dialogue conveys the speaker, the listener and the context – just as much as it conveys the sense.

'Register' is a concept described by linguists and familiar to actors. It is an element of English usage that we all employ instinctively, though most of us are not consciously aware of what we do. Put simply, the 'register' of any utterance or piece of writing is the degree of complexity of the vocabulary and grammar it employs. Educated speakers select the register automatically depending on the audience and the context. As an example, a husband might use a different register talking to his wife, depending on whether they are at home, in the street, or participating in a public meeting.

There are generally considered to be five such registers, ranging from one (the lowest) through to five, though we shall be chiefly concerned with the three middle ones. The written register appropriate to a context is always a level higher than the spoken one, because intonation and facial expression are no longer available to help convey the sense.

Level one – the lowest **'intimate' register** – is only possible in speech, so you won't be writing it (though you may pretend to be doing so, as we shall see). It relies on intonation and shared experience. There is little formal grammatical structure. Utterances may consist of single words or even a private language with invented vocabulary and its own grammar rules. Communication relies on the participants sharing so much common knowledge that what is said is just a prompt. New information is well-nigh impossible, so even intimates cannot keep this register up for very long.

'Casual' English is the second register and, as the name suggests, is used between friends and acquaintances when the context is 'casual'. This is the style of conversation you might overhear on public transport, for example. People are not conveying important information but exchanging pleasantries, gossiping or confirming what the other person already knows. Subject pronouns (I, he, we, etc.) are often missing, or moved to the end of sentences ('Fed up, I am!'). Verbs are contracted (haven't, aren't, shouldn't've) and sentences are simple and often incomplete. There may be grammatical mistakes. There are not many adjectives, apart from basic things like colour, age and size. There are, however, often 'strengtheners' (often grammatical adverbs, but sometimes swear words) which are actually not doing much except to emphasize or, more commonly, exaggerate: 'Bought hisself a bloody great car down that poncy garage, you know where I mean.'

Other adverbs are rare in this register. There may be dialect words and slang but precise, technical expressions are avoided. What look like explanations usually are not – 'Why? Because I said so.'

This kind of dialogue is a vital tool for crime fiction writers. It indicates informality, so it suggests an attitude, and it is the perfect way to introduce such things as names. Have confidence to use it – in the proper context it is actually 'correct'. Here you can hide your vital 'throwaways' (see above). Don't let it actually ramble, though. Aim to achieve maximum effect in the fewest words.

The third level register is called the **'informative' register,** and you can see that you are going to have to write a lot of that in crime fiction. Most of the explanation and witness statements will have to be couched in this register. Fortunately, there are two subdivision here, which gives the advantage of variety.

- **'Informal information'register** – where sentences are generally complete and more or less grammatical. Here are a full range of non-technical adjectives, adverbs of time and manner (e.g. 'often' and 'beautifully') and even subordinate clauses beginning with 'that', 'which' and 'who' – for example, 'She's the woman who lives in that house next to the pub.' There may be simple explanations, using expressions like 'because it was raining', but precise technical expressions are replaced by deliberately vaguer ones. There are made-up expressions in the dictionary which were created specifically for this: a thingummy, a whatyoumacallit, a doofer. Note that the speaker may well know the proper term, but is instinctively avoiding it because of the degree of formality in the interaction. A lot of witness testimony will be couched in this register.

- **'Instructive information' register** – here the whole structure and vocabulary is more formal and complex. Proper technical terms are used, sentences are longer and grammar is correct. The speaker has thought through in detail the sense of what they mean to say, though without necessarily planning the exact words they mean to use. This is the way explanatory talks are generally delivered and formal interrogation sometimes calls for it. For example: 'So tell us, Mrs Blake, in your own words if you would, exactly what happened yesterday when you encountered this stranger in your drive.'

Snapshot exercise

Look at that last sentence again. You can see that 'Mrs Blake', whoever she may be, will be put at an immediate disadvantage if she only usually operates in a lower register, though she may not necessarily be aware of this. Look at this possible reply: 'Well, it's like this, inspector. My son, see – 'e works down the Co-op, helps them stack the shelves. 'e gen'rally comes in about that time of day. Well, thought it was him first, didn't I?'

- What register would you say that Mrs Blake was using here?
- Is it appropriate?
- Based on this exchange, what do you assume about her social standing, her age, her degree of education and her character?
- Where do you suppose that this taking is place?
- What gives you that impression?

Write a sentence or two describing the participants as you imagine them. Please note that this isn't typecasting. Speech – like physical description – is one of the ways in which we judge the people that we meet. It is a writer's tool and can convey a great deal within a paragraph or two. Try to make your dialogue work for you in this way.

E.O. Wilson

'I've found that good dialogue tells you not only what people are saying or how they're communicating but it tells you a great deal – by dialect and tone, content and circumstance – about the quality of the character.'

Edit exercise

Look back at the 'interrogation' scene that you wrote for the last chapter. What alterations would you make to it, if any, in light of what you now know about register? Try redrafting.

The fourth register is the so-called **'formal register'** and is rarely used in speech. It occurs where people have thought through in advance precisely the words they mean to use. Even when it is spoken, it is often written first – as in a speech or lecture – or at least mentally rehearsed (as in the case of a prepared answer at a job interview). There's no discursion or deviation. There is usually a wide vocabulary, with the full range of possible adverbs, adjectives and clauses of all sorts, and sentences may be twice as long as in other registers. Don't let your characters talk like this, unless you want them to sound unpleasantly cold or pedantic (which you may of course – the most chilling threats are sometimes issued in this register). Autocue writers for TV understand this perfectly and build in moments of 'spontaneity'.

The fifth or **'literary' register** need not concern us, and I include it only for the sake of completeness. Here the words are not only thought out in advance but carefully revised so that every syllable is chosen for maximum effect. Poetry is the obvious example here, though other writers may aspire to it. It is not usually applicable to crime and thriller genres.

So this is your challenge when writing dialogue. You are aware that you are writing prose, so often the instinct is to follow the unspoken rules of register and make your exchanges conform to the 'formal' style, which is normally appropriate for any written English (other than a personal letter or a note). But nobody – repeat nobody – really talks that way. You are attempting to capture level two or three (or even register one, if you are writing about lovers) so you have deliberately to imitate features of those registers. However, your reader also knows that this is written English, so you can't entirely abandon the conventions that apply to it. In real conversation people may make errors of grammar all the time, drop every 'h' and get their words mixed up. If you do that in your novel, it will look overdone. What you want are a few careful cues.

Write now

If you are working on a novel of your own by now, take two of your own characters and see whether you can write a short scene in which the two of them appear. (Don't make it an interrogation dialogue involving the sleuth this time – though if you have made your sleuth your viewpoint character they may have to appear.) Aim to have at least a third of the scene as dialogue and try to ensure that the episode also moves the plot along.

If you are not yet working on a novel, use two of the 'suspect' characters you created earlier – perhaps discussing the discovery of the corpse and revealing some more of that biography you wrote before. Or take the story forward in any way you like.

Why each character should have a different 'voice'

In real life every person has a distinctive 'voice', depending on their background, age and education, and the same should be true for all your characters. Of course, you cannot indicate the timbre of their speech but you can capture a tone, indicate the diction and catch the turn of phrase. It should be possible to work out who the speaker is, even without the 'speech directions', if you get this right. Do make sure that all the voices are not all simply yours – you aren't the same age and background as all your characters. Young people speak differently from older ones – listen to people in public places, and note down words and phrases that seem 'typical' of different groups.

Focus point

Make sure that each major character has a distinctive voice – and that it's not the same as yours.

There are tricks for differentiating speakers. Here are some of them:

- **Use a slightly different register for each major character.** Remember that too much formality creates a pompous bore; also that the register a person chooses when talking, for instance to someone in authority, indicates the speaker's attitude to that authority.
- **Choose your vocabulary with care.** This is where your eavesdropping comes in.
- **Don't be afraid to use slang and blasphemy** if that's what your characters would say. However, do it very sparingly. Swearing and profanity are very strong in print (because it is a written register, where these things don't belong) and too much can disturb the balance of the dialogue.

Key idea

Low life does not speak like high life – and even high life probably doesn't speak the way you think it does.

- If you are writing about people much older or younger than yourself, listen to people of that age group carefully. The idiom they use won't be the same as yours. Don't, however, be tempted by the very latest teenage slang and jargon – nothing dates a book more quickly than yesterday's street language.
- Read your dialogue aloud as if it were a play. Try to listen to the different voices in your head. It will soon be obvious if it doesn't work as speech.
- Suggest a dialect or accent, where appropriate. Again, don't overdo it. Don't drop every aspirate or write 'begorrah!' every line or two – one suggestion per paragraph is probably enough.
- Use what you now know about mental processes (see Chapter 2 on settings). Make one major character use visual imagery, another talk about what they hear, let a third give precise dimensions and use figures constantly, while another majors on 'touchy-feely' things. This is probably the easiest of all techniques, largely because the reader won't even notice it.
- Deliberately change the rhythm of the words for different speakers. Give one longer sentences or shorter words. This can be difficult at first, because you will have a normal rhythm of speech. Try tapping out the stresses to find out what it is – and then deliberately override it for your least attractive characters. Your readers will not be consciously aware of it, but a rhythm different from the connecting prose will set up a feeling of unease.
- Answer a question with a question now and then. This is particularly good for confrontational exchanges. For example, 'Who was that girl?', 'What girl?', 'You know perfectly well what girl. Do you think I'm blind as well as stupid?'
- When you have written a piece of dialogue, use the 'tagless' test. Tags are 'speech instructions' about who is saying what (like 'Fred said' and 'Judith asked'). Take them out and see whether it is still clear who the speaker is.

Edit exercise

Choose either of the pieces of dialogue that you wrote earlier. Apply the 'tagless' test to it – do the speakers remain totally distinct? Even if they do, try mentally applying the techniques suggested – perhaps in different paragraphs of the exchange – so that you become familiar with them all. When you are confident, rewrite the dialogue incorporating any useful changes.

Managing the voice for a viewpoint character

We talked in the last chapter about the 'viewpoint' character, and their 'uncensored' thoughts. If we are in the mind of a viewpoint character, then we are 'listening' to their inner voice, which should be similar in tone and vocabulary to the dialogue they speak. In fact, this is usually the way we recognize whose viewpoint we are in.

- The way people talk to others betrays their attitude and personality. If you wish to make your character seem friendly and relaxed, use the trappings of a 'casual' register – incomplete sentences, contractions, slang and so on. If you want a boring pedant, write convoluted sentences full of fancy words.

- Whatever you choose, make sure that idioms and vocabulary match the background and life experience of the character, and are not simply those that you, yourself, would use.

- There is an additional device available to your viewpoint character: quoting the words of another speaker – more or less verbatim, but not in direct speech. This suggests that the narrator has an attitude, is worried, amused or cynically unimpressed by what was said. Look at the next Snapshot exercise to see this in action. Be careful to keep the quoted register and voice appropriate.

- If you are writing historical crime, the rules are different. For example, Jane Austen's ladies called their husbands 'Mr So-and-so'. Modern register is generally more casual than it used to be. But this is a little like writing dialect: don't write the whole of your dialogue like this, or your manuscript will be unreadable. Add just a hint or two per paragraph.

Snapshot exercise

Look again at that short scene from *Resurrection Men* (repeated here for your convenience).

Her name was Andrea Thomson. She wasn't a doctor – she'd made that clear at their first meeting. Nor was she a 'shrink' or 'therapist'. 'Career analysis' was what it had said on Rebus's daily sheet. 2:30–3:15: Career analysis. Rm3.16

With Ms Thomson. Which had become Andrea at the moment of introduction. Which was yesterday. Tuesday. A 'get-to-know' session, she'd called it.

She was in her late thirties, short and large-hipped. Her hair was a thick mop of blond with some darker streaks showing through. Her teeth were slightly oversized. She was self-employed, didn't work for the police full-time.

'Do any of us?' Rebus had asked yesterday. She'd looked a bit puzzled.

Ian Rankin, *Resurrection Men*

What did Andrea actually say at the first meeting with Rebus yesterday? Try writing that scene as a piece of dialogue. Why do you think Rankin opted not to use this more direct technique? Who is the 'viewpoint character' here?

One of the clearest indications that you've switched viewpoint character is the change of 'voice' – signalled by a change of vocabulary, length of sentence and so on. If you have two viewpoint characters whose backgrounds and therefore written 'voices' aren't particularly distinct, try giving one a little mannerism (nothing elaborate, just the habit of occasionally closing utterances with 'eh?', for instance) and aim to avoid making those two viewpoints consecutive.

Using dialogue to speed or slow the action

Speech is a kind of action in itself, albeit sometimes a fairly static one. People are doing something when they talk. That means that you have characters involved.

Key idea

Dialogue is literally action of a kind. Your characters are doing something – speaking in this case.

- Use this to your advantage by breaking up long paragraphs of connective prose with just a word or two of dialogue. This can even add to tension at dramatic moments – 'Listen! What was that?' – one reason why it's useful to have a sidekick for your sleuth!
- And vice versa. Break up long passages of dialogue with physical action of some kind. However, beware of merely stroking chins and clearing throats. Try to make this action useful in some way, such as reminding the reader what the setting is, planting a throwaway, introducing a red herring or quietly furthering the plot.

- Make it a rule never to have one person speaking for too long at once. If you have different voices, even a change of speaker is a change of pace.
- You can increase tension by having an important interchange interrupted at a crucial point – but use this device with care. Once in your first novel is enough, and don't repeat it for a book or two! Readers will notice if you overdo this trick.
- Ensure that your exchange is grounded in a scene. Everything happens somewhere, so write in little pointers in between the speech. (If we are in a restaurant, let your people eat; if in a car, make sure that they brake or stop at traffic lights.) It will stop your characters becoming 'talking heads' and give your dialogue variety.
- Mysteries often involve a lot of verbal explanation at the end. Make sure that you break this up sufficiently. This is a moment for as much external action as you can introduce (even questions and reactions from other characters), to keep the reader engaged. Make the explanation as snappy as you can – or contrive to break it into separate scenes, revealing a portion of the answer in each one. Poirot-type finales (where all the characters are gathered in the drawing room and he explains the possible motives of them all before revealing what actually occurred) are no longer viable.

Write now

Write a page of dialogue for your novel as before, this time another interrogation featuring your sleuth, but making it as different in nature from the last one as you can. Or if you intend to write thrillers, write a dialogue in which the victim discovers the nature of the threat – using a phone conversation if you wish, but not involving data sent by text or Internet. If you don't have a plot outline in mind yet, use Mrs Blake and the inspector, inventing the circumstances as you go along. (The plotline doesn't really matter for this exercise.) Pay particular attention to the register, breaking up the paragraphs and keeping the dialogue grounded in the scene.

Technical things to bear in mind when writing direct speech

- **Get the punctuation right.** This matters. Nothing looks more amateur than mispunctuated speech. If you do not understand the rules, get hold of a good manual and learn them now. It isn't really complicated. The Appendix to this book will give you a few suggestions for helpful texts on this.

- **Don't have people tell other people things that they already know,** or otherwise say unlikely things, simply to pass on background information to the reader. For example, 'Let's call our sixteen-year-old son Tom down for tea. He is upstairs in this charming Victorian cottage by the lake.' (Exaggerated? You would be surprised what people write! Just be sure that you don't do this yourself!)
- **Names are an easy way of suggesting register and the degree of familiarity between two characters.** Think of a character called Jennifer. Who calls her Jen? Jenny? Poppet? Mrs Blake?
- **Cut out the adverbs telling the reader how the words were said** unless they are really essential to the sense. If you've caught the voice, you won't need most of them. We'll return to this a little later in the book.
- **Don't bother with looking for alternatives to 'said'.** In dialogue that word is near-invisible. If you have your characters 'declaiming', 'declaring' or 'stating' constantly, the reader's attention is distracted to the verb. Similarly, save words like 'hissing', 'spitting' and 'murmuring' for moments when it really matters.
- **You can avoid writing speech directions for every utterance anyway.** Remember the tag test? If the dialogue is right, we recognize the voice. Insert an action by the speaker, and you don't need 'said'. This speeds up the narrative as well. For example:

'Give me that knife!' He stretched out a hand.

Focus point

Keep speech directions simple.

Workshop exercise

Here is part of the opening scene of a crime thriller.

'You've been shot,' Rygg stated.

The man just stared at him.

'I'll get help,' Rygg said, but the man, with a grimace stretched out the hand of his wounded arm towards him.

'Please reach into the breast pocket of my shirt and take out my cigarettes,' he said. His accent was a little too

rounded to be English and his voice seemed far too steady for a man who'd just been shot. Rygg did as he asked. They were cheap Gauloises. The lighter was in the pocket. He placed a cigarette between the man's lips and lit it.

'Now I'm going to get someone,' Rygg said.

'Please, sir, if you want to help me you will not do so.'

'Look, you've just been shot in the arm. You're lucky you're alive – that woman's dead, I think!' He pointed to the square. 'But you need to stop the bleeding and get some stitches. I'll stay with you if you need me.'

'You are a tourist?' the man asked unexpectedly.

'Yes, here on business but mixing it with some pleasure.'

'You are staying in a hotel?'

'The Crillon-Hapsburg. On …'

'Hasselbrookstrasse. I know it. Please. If you want to help me, take me to your room. For one hour. Not more. You will be recompensed.'

Martin Molsted, *Chasing the Storm*

Look at the dialogue. Which of the techniques outlined in this chapter has the author used? How does he indicate the non-Englishness of the man who has been shot? If you took out the speech directions would you still know who was saying what? Do any of the speech directions interrupt the flow?

(The author of this extract is Scandinavian. If he can do it, you can!)

Where to next?

We have seen that dialogue springs from character, and characters from settings. These ingredients, however, do not make a book, any more than separate cake ingredients become a cake. It requires you to 'mix' them and make them interact. People give you motives, events create a plot. We will look at this in Chapter 5.

5

Plotting and structure

How, and to what degree, you plan a crime novel will probably be down to your preferred writing practices. In this chapter, however, you fill some important pointers as to how you can create a strong, engaging structure for your book that will keep your readers reading from beginning to end, especially in the middle, which is where things can get dull.

Where do writers get their plot lines from?

They make them up. If you are a crime novelist, this is your job – to find ideas and make a plot from them.

It's often said that there are stories everywhere, but – as usual – that's not so true for crime. Murder is rare and crime-thriller-type threats and abductions rarer still. Besides, true crime is often very dull (from an author's point of view) and – worse – predictable. Nine-tenths of real murder is committed by someone in the victim's household, for motives too banal to make a mystery. And you're not writing true crime anyway – you're a novelist!

For crime stories, everyday life offers only the potential of a plot. But there's a lot of that. Read your local newspaper. Who was sent to prison for attacking whom and why? Who is embroiled in a terrible divorce? Who finds that they are ruined, and by whom? Who is troubled by a stalker? You don't want those actual people in your book, of course – but these events may give you the seedlings of a plot.

And it doesn't have to be a newspaper: any unusual occurrence can lead you to ideas. If something's noteworthy enough to make your friends and neighbours talk, it is likely to support an interesting plot. Just ensure that the drives and motives fit your characters and the setting and background from which they emerge.

Better still, just turn your mental TV on, tune in to your characters and watch how they behave. When you get skilled at that, you'll know who murders whom. Imagination is the most precious tool you have.

 Stephen King

'There is no Idea Dump, no Story Central, no Island of the Buried Bestsellers. Your job isn't to find these ideas, but to recognize them when they show up.'

The built-in structure of crime fiction and how that can help

Something available to crime writers, though – more than to writers of any other genre – is a built-in structure for a book. The conventions of crime fiction require a certain basic pattern in the narrative. You can express this as a series of questions, and when you've answered them, you already have a framework for your plot.

- Who killed (or intends to kill or threaten) whom – why, how, where and when?
- How is this discovered?
- What is the result?
- Who else is affected, threatened or involved?
- What sort of person was the murderer? Or, if you plan a thriller, what motivates the threat?
- What sort of person was the victim/corpse?
- What sort of person solved or prevented the crime?
- What wrong turns, if any, did the investigation take?
- Who, apart from the murderer, had anything to hide?
- What is different about this episode/murder that interests me? (If you aren't interested yourself, why should your reader be?)

Snapshot exercise

Think back to any crime novel (or full-length TV crime drama) you have recently enjoyed. Answer the questions in the previous paragraph in relation to that story. Write your answers down, so that you have something to compare with later on. If you can do this for more than one subgenre – a thriller and a whodunnit, for example – you may find this helpful in understanding the built-in structure of a plot.

The rules – or lack of them – for writing plots

Beyond this helpful framework, there are no rules at all – especially in the way that writers plot their books.

- Some people plan in detail – I have a friend whose wall is full of charts showing a careful outline of what happens in every chapter before she starts to write.
- Other people start with just a core idea – usually about the central crime and how it is resolved – then 'set people off and see what happens', as Margaret Yorke once memorably said.
- Most writers operate between the two extremes, with a vague cast of characters, a solution in mind, and a notional outline of the plot, but allow themselves the freedom to change things as they go.

- Probably as a beginner you will find it best to sketch out some sort of plan, with an idea of what key events are going to happen, and when. But don't let that become a straitjacket once you start to write. Your characters may have their own ideas (an indication that they're becoming nicely real) or something better may strike as you go along. If that happens, experiment a bit. If it doesn't work, reject it and go back to what you planned.

There are, though, a few 'no-no' conventions of the 'whodunnit' genre – things that it is better to avoid. There are several lists of these (made long ago and partly tongue-in-cheek) but they still represent sound advice – with the inevitable exceptions! So here goes, with apologies to Ronald Knox and S.S. Van Dine.

- No elaborate disguises involving masks, prosthetic features or facial surgery. Hair dye and sunglasses are just permissible.
- No identical twins or secret passages (though you will find some of these in classic works!).
- No poisons previously unknown to science or cunning new appliances that require a lengthy explanation at the end.
- Don't have your murder committed by shifty foreigners (except in spy/crime thrillers or realistic crime).
- Avoid posh country houses, hunt balls and tennis parties (unless you're setting your story in the 1930s or earlier).
- Don't let the sleuth do it (unless you're Agatha Christie or your readers already know the character from previous books – in which case you're published and don't need my advice).

The comic crime genre does not observe these 'rules'. There these 'no-nos' frequently occur as part of the joke, which shows why it's better to avoid them if you're writing 'serious' crime.

Where to start your novel

🔑 Key idea

Start with the crime (or the threat, in thriller mode), not the backstory that led up to it.

New novelists often start with background information. Don't do that in crime. You can build that all in later – that is what witnesses and confidants are for.

- Make sure that the crime or the threat (in a thriller) happens – or is at least suspected – by the end of the first chapter at the latest.
- Put your murdered body in the first sentence, if you like. Shock openings work very well in mysteries. But you can't repeat this in every book you write and it doesn't suit all plots anyway. So use the exercises here to experiment with different ways of opening your tale.
- Or lull the reader with tranquillity for a page or two, and then destroy it with a nasty crime. Lots of psychological whydunniits and thrillers work like this.
- You can use the 'moment of inquietude' technique in your opening paragraphs. This is where no threat or crime has actually occurred but the author sows the seed of something being not quite right. This can be physical – a character glimpses someone in the crowd, whose funeral he attended a year or two before – or suggestion only – 'Anna slowed her jogging pace and glanced around. There it was again, that uneasy feeling that she was being watched.'
- Or start with the reader knowing something that the character does not. This may be subtle, like seeing the prospective victim through the would-be killer's/abductor's eyes, for example, 'She was the sort of girl that made his pulses race. Blonde hair, blue eyes, incipient little breasts. Just like the others. And he'd have this one, too. But this time he wouldn't kill her. Not at first, at least.' Or by direct author comment: 'As Anna battled on to the 8.30 commuter train to work, she didn't know that by this evening she'd be dead.'

Snapshot exercise

Try writing an opening for a crime story you know, employing one of the techniques above. When you've finished, compare it with the original if possible.

Next time you read a crime novel, watch out for these techniques and make a note of any that you find especially effective.

- In whodunnits, introduce your sleuth and villain early on. The sleuth should appear in the first chapter, and the killer by the fourth at the latest, as a rule. If the murderer has not appeared by then, the reader cannot begin to work out who it is – and for at least half the readership, that is half the fun.
- Add a good distracter of some kind, too, where that's applicable, as soon as possible.

Workshop exercise

We can learn a lot from looking at the plot and structure of classic fairy tales. Here is an example of a 'thriller' of a kind.

Once there was a little girl named Red Riding Hood. She lived in a thick forest where her father was a woodcutter. One day her mother said to her, 'Take this basket of fresh cakes to your grandmother, who is ill in bed, but don't wander off the forest path or talk to any strangers on the way!'

Little Red Riding Hood said, 'I won't,' and hurried off. But on her way she saw some flowers growing amid the trees. 'Just that little way off the path won't hurt,' she thought. She went to pick some for her grandmother.

The Big Bad Wolf was hiding in the woods. When he saw the little girl he hurried up to her. He smiled, thinking what a tasty meal she would make. 'What's your name, little girl?'

'Little Red Riding Hood,' she said.

'Those are lovely flowers.' He licked his lips and smiled.

'They're for my grandmother. She is ill in bed. I'm taking this basket of fresh cakes to her. She lives in the cottage at the far side of the wood.'

Two meals, thought the Big Bad Wolf. 'Then I mustn't keep you!' He waved goodbye and ran off into the wood. He hurried to the grandmother's cottage and knocked on the door.

'It's Red Riding Hood,' he said, trying to sound as much like her as he could. 'I've brought a basket of fresh cakes for you.'

'Come in,' said the old woman. 'The door is on the latch.'

The wolf rushed in and grabbed the grandmother. There was no time to eat her straight away, so he pushed her in the cupboard and locked the door. Then he put her nightcap on, and lay down in the bed, pulling the bedclothes up around his chin. A moment afterwards, Red Riding Hood arrived. She hurried to the bed.

'Why, Grandmother,' she cried, 'what big eyes you have!'

'All the better to see you with, my dear!' replied the wolf.

'But, Grandmother, what big ears you have!'

'All the better to hear you with, my dear!'

'And, Grandmother, what big teeth you have!'

'All the better to eat you with, my dear!'

He pushed back the covers and jumped out of bed. Red Riding Hood realized that it was the wolf. She let out a frightful scream. Luckily the woodcutter was working close by. He heard the scream and came running, just in time. With his woodman's axe he chopped up the Big Bad Wolf, then opened the cupboard and rescued Grandmother. And they sat and ate the cakes.

They all lived happily ever afterwards – though Red Riding Hood never wandered from the path or spoke to strangers in the wood again.

Look at the structure of the story. Where does it begin? How much 'back story' is included at the start?

Where is the first indication of danger – the first explicit threat? Where is the threat deliberately 'held back', because the reader knows what the character does not? Can you write this as a series of plot points?

There are two major scenes in the story. What are they devoted to?

Whose story is it? Who else's point of view are we given? Can you see that we have the classic victim–threat alternating viewpoints of thriller fiction here?

In some versions of the story the wolf eats the grandmother, and sometimes the woodcutter is not mentioned until the end. How do these variations affect the story?

In Perrault's original the girl is eaten, too. The woodcutter has to rescue them from the stomach of the wolf and replace them with stones while the creature is asleep, so that the wolf will drown when he goes to drink. Why do you think this ancient folk version has not survived so well?

Planning the end

Key idea

A successful resolution depends on effort of some kind.

This is true for almost every genre, but in crime fiction especially. Here's why. Your characters must work either to solve the crime, or prevent it, and do so in ways that your readers can follow, and with which they empathize. The goal is to make the reader imagine that – given the opportunity – they could do the same thing with the same result. Otherwise they'll feel cheated and your book will not succeed.

ENDING A WHODUNNIT OR A MYSTERY

Make sure that your characters earn the solution that you've arranged for them, by contributing to it. The effort may be mental (working out the clues) or physical (especially in realistic crime) or any combination of the two. But effort must be there. Chance and coincidence are not enough. Nor is intuition not based on clues and facts. Above all, don't have intervention from the spirit world, even if your story is set in ancient Egypt. Your sleuth may half suspect the gods have helped, but modern readers must believe he did it by himself.

 P.D. James

'[The mystery] is solved not by good luck or divine intervention, it's solved by a human being. By human courage and human intelligence and human perseverance. In a sense, the detective story is a small celebration of reason and order in our very disorderly world.'

ENDINGS IN CRIME THRILLERS

Much the same is true for the crime thriller. We have to see the effort made to thwart the criminal or avert the threat. And we need to watch it happen. Someone coming forward to explain how they were kidnapped is not a story – it is either the beginning or the end of one: the beginning if the kidnapper has now disappeared, the end if it's the victim's story and the escape or rescue is the result of the 'effort'.

COMIC CRIME

This is the grand exception. Here the idiot often stumbles on the answer by sheer chance, or foils a murder by blundering into it, succeeding by sheer ineptitude. In every other version of the genre, effort is a must.

WRITING THE LAST FEW PAGES – ALL SUBGENRES

The end of the plot is the solution of the crime or, in thrillers, the rescue of the victim and the removal of the threat. Full stop. However, that is not usually the best way to conclude. Plan to add a little extra at the end – often a tiny scene resolving a romance, or a comic moment, or anything to show that surviving characters have lives that carry on. Think of any crime fiction film you've ever seen, and you'll recognize the device. This is not just a sentimental 'feel-good' strategy – sometimes called a 'goodnight, John-Boy' moment – it has a function. It ensures that the reader has time to mentally 'catch up' before they shut the book. Without this – and it should not be more than a page or two at most – the end may seem abrupt. This can leave the reader (or editor) a bit dissatisfied, often without quite understanding why.

Write now

So it's your turn. By now you should have a list of motives, a setting and potential characters. These are the raw materials for a crime novel. All you need now is to decide which of your suspects did it, who your sleuth is going to be, what clues will lead them to the truth and what wrong turnings they will take meanwhile.

Sketch out a plot line for a novel using these ingredients, breaking it into likely chapters as you go. Aim for 15 chapters as a minimum. If you are working on a novel of your own, by all means use that for this exercise. If you find this task difficult, do your best with it, but don't be afraid to leave a chapter blank if you really can't decide what ought to go in it. We'll look at further strategies when you know what you require.

P.S. If you've got interested in that body by the wall, or any of the other three scenarios, then stick with it. Write it if you want to. Sell it if you can. It's yours. No one else who does this exercise is going to write the same story as you do, even if the starting point is the same.

The 'clothes line' effect

So you have the starting point and the solution is plotted in your mind. (You probably need at least this, before you start to write.) That's the easy part. Between the beginning and the end we need sufficient tension to keep the reader hooked. Think of an old-fashioned clothes line. The starting point and the solution are the events – the props – that hold up your narrative at either end. Your task is to keep the line from getting slack between the two.

 ## Mickey Spillane

Nobody reads a mystery to get to the middle. They read it to get to the end.

Many beginners' manuscripts begin to sag halfway, because the author has not built in sufficient 'tensioners' on the way. Make a deliberate effort to add them as you go. Think of these as extra 'clothes props' inserted now and then, to keep the narrative line taut.

 ## Focus point

Make sure that your story has tension in the middle. Have interesting things happening throughout, not just at either end.

There are several ways of doing this:

- Identify exciting moments in the plot and space them out. Don't have all the action happening at once. After a violent or dramatic scene, let your reader have a page or two of hope or rest – bizarrely this will keep the tension up. But stick to just a page or two. Allow the readership just enough time to begin to think they can relax, and then sock them again.
- Make sure that there are at least three major incidents. Really major ones. These may even be more murders (check how many whodunnits have three corpses by the end). Or they may be moments of danger to the sleuth – someone tries to kill them, or sets fire to their office to destroy the evidence. Have one of these major incidents at the beginning, one roughly one-third through, and the last between the two-thirds and three-quarters point. As you learn to do this, you can vary these ratios of course, but this is a useful beginner's rule.
- These core events not only keep the tension high, they change the focus and break the story up. Try to make each incident come as a surprise – this is always good for maintaining interest.

Sometimes it can also inject some urgency, for example if the sleuth must solve the problem before other people die.

- In the same way, in a thriller, we may have several foiled attempts at abduction of the victim, or a 'warning' crime where a different victim dies. Each 'horrible example' of what might happen next makes the need for rescue more vivid and more tense. But don't overdo it: three is quite enough.

- Identify important low points and space those, too. Low points are the moments when the hero-protagonist temporarily fails. A favoured theory is proved completely wrong, they devote a whole day to following false leads, or arrive at the crime scene to find the hoped-for witnesses have fled. Or, in a thriller, someone rushes off to save the victim from a threatened kidnapping, only to discover it's too late – she's gone. Low points of this kind – because they come about when hope is dashed – are sometimes referred to as 'false dawns'.

- These low points are often mental ones, but can include external happenings: a suspect steals a vital photograph, a crucial journey is delayed by fog, or a simple puncture ruins a chase, meaning that a suspect gets away. Again, it is important to space these throughout the book, preferably between the major incidents – they are also 'clothes props' in their way. But don't have too many – two or three such setbacks are enough – and be sure to give them different forms. If your hero is perpetually foiled by accidents – or repeats the same mistakes – your readers will start to think he/she is unintelligent and, unless you're writing comic crime, lose patience with the plot.

- Having a low point closely followed by a high point is more effective than the other way about.

These strategies should give you a number of 'prop' ideas, but you'll need more than that. Here are some other lesser tricks that you can use:

- Physical action, especially violent, keeps the plot alive, even when the sleuth is just a bystander. If your scene is getting dull, make two people have a fight – preferably suspects, and for a reason connected with the plot. A pair of women pulling out each other's hair, because the wife has just discovered that there has been an affair, will liven up a tedious piece of sleuthing wonderfully.

If you do write such a scene, here is a useful trick. Immediately before the fight, disclose a vital clue. The reader will probably forget it, because attention becomes focused on the brawl.

'In writing a novel, when in doubt, have two guys come through the door with guns.'

- Introducing a fresh character will add new interest. Obviously this is easiest early in the book – you don't want important characters to turn up very late. But your investigator – having found a name – can search for that person unsuccessfully. When that character eventually appears (through the efforts of the sleuth or of their team, for preference), anticipation will have doubled the effect.
- Introducing a new location can be a minor 'prop' if the place is striking and very different. Sometimes these last two strategies go hand in hand – the missing person turns up in a squalid slum, in a splendid Scottish parsonage or a boathouse on Lake Tahoe – whatever gives you contrast and fits the character.
- Use these strategies in the subplot too, for a less striking version of the same effect. That is partly what a subplot is for.

Key idea

Don't allow yourself to write a whole chapter without some 'clothes-prop' in it to keep the interest up.

Using 'What if…' questions to sustain a plot

You may have encountered this advice. You ask yourself a question and the story answers it. In a sense, it is exactly what fiction is all about. Your whole plot is a sort of 'What if…?' exercise. (What if there was a body lying by a wall?) There are moments, though, when you can use it consciously:

- If you come to a standstill halfway through the plot, and need to decide what ought to happen next, ask yourself some 'What if…' questions on the scene so far. What if your character isn't what he seems? What if he knows a secret about the next person he meets? What if his ex-lover suddenly walked in? Think of half-a-dozen questions, but don't write anything. Try the different scenarios in your head. It is likely that one will strike a chord, or start another, different train of thought.

- If none of them succeeds in doing that, ask yourself the cruellest question of them all: what if that last event hadn't happened as you've written it? If you are prepared to scrap a page or two, you may suddenly see what the next step ought to be. Note: We are talking only about plotting here – keeping up the 'clothes line' in between key incidents. We'll look a little later at ways of overcoming more general writer's block.

Jeffery Deaver

'I've often said that there's no such thing as writer's block; the problem is idea block. When I find myself frozen… it's usually because I'm trying to shoehorn an idea into the passage or story where it has no place.'

- You can write some 'What if…' questions when you're working well so you've got them to turn to when you reach a block. Make them random, tie them to the plot or base them on the latest newspaper. Or base them on the theme, as we shall below. This technique works very well for subplots, in particular.
- If no subplot suggests itself to you, go back to the setting and the characters that you've created in your head. Make one character simply walk along and ask 'What if…' questions as you visualize the scene. (What if she has a secret? What if she had a child when she was young? What if it suddenly turned up again today?) Keep on asking 'What ifs' with each character, until a useful thought occurs to you.

Focus point

All plots are really 'What if…' questions answered in some way.

The place of a theme in crime writing

It is often said that mainstream novels have a theme as well as a plot, though this does not apply to crime as much. But it can be useful to identify a theme, especially if you find it difficult to write subplots otherwise.

- If you had no theme in mind at all, begin by thinking of the seven deadly sins. Could your theme be 'greed/lust/wrath/envy does not pay'? Or does one of the 'virtues' triumph – love, loyalty, honesty or truth?

- Sometimes a maxim will offer you a theme – 'all power corrupts', or 'Aztecs were people very much like us'.

- The nature of justice is a common theme in crime. Try 'justice will triumph', or even 'good will out'.

- Some modern novels have the offender get away, simply driven down again 'until next time'. If this is you, your theme could be expressed as 'you can overcome evil for a time, but not destroy it'.

- It is sometimes useful to identify the 'theme' in writing a proposal.

- If you haven't got a side-plot and need one, try working in another variation on your theme, for instance a different kind of lust or greed. This is not only a source of new ideas, it will give the book coherence.

- Once your thriller villain has been introduced, and you have a lot of neutral narrative to write, try making that character flout the theme in lots of little ways. If your theme is 'honesty' and they are walking down the road, have them cheat a passing child, or steal a paper from a newsvendor. If you're with the victim's viewpoint, do the opposite. These moments drive the narrative along, even when not much else is happening.

But remember, the theme should *never* dominate your book. You are writing entertainment, not a moral treatise. The theme emerges from the story that you tell – it isn't something that you write your plot to demonstrate.

The role of subplots

Subplots are important to successful crime stories. Mystery stories half depend on them, as each red herring is a side-plot on its own. Events in the subplot can be used as props to keep pace and interest up when the main plot is suspended or getting a bit dull. Also, you can hide important clues to the central mystery (instance an allusion to who was where and when) in 'conversation' between subplot players, where they appear to be talking about their own affairs.

SUBPLOTS IN MYSTERIES

People often appear guilty for reasons unconnected with the central plot. Suspects may lie in talking to the sleuth to protect themselves or someone else. Each of these reasons is a story in itself – think of these as little subplots and use them accordingly. Space high and low moments in them to 'prop' the narrative.

There may be a subplot connected with the sleuth, in police procedurals especially. It may concern private or professional relationships, or even a minor case that runs in parallel, though it helps if this has tangential relevance to the central plot. (He is called away from dealing with a street-gang incident with local hoodies wielding a knife. His remaining colleagues confiscate the blade. This later proves to be the murder weapon he is looking for – the hoodies found it hidden in a hedge and it's been in police possession ever since.)

SUBPLOTS IN THRILLERS

Here subplots generally revolve only around the central characters. The focus is on the intended crime, and other people's interests only interrupt. Victim or rescuer (or both) may have a personal crisis, which creates a sub-story. This may be a romance, a marriage placed at risk, or even a medical emergency (mother falls downstairs and has been rushed to hospital, the children have a soaring temperature, or if the victim doesn't get her insulin, she'll die). Whatever it is, it should be emotional and pressing. Faced with real danger, nothing else is a legitimate concern.

This subplot must affect the outcome in some way: delay the rescue, interfere with the solution of the crime, intensify the risk, or add mental anguish to the victim's suffering. Used like this, a subplot can drive the plot along.

Focus point

Subplots are what give a story depth.

Edit exercise

Look at the plot line you created earlier. What are the potential subplots? If you haven't got any, try to add some now. Look at the suggested uses of such plots and if you have 'thin' chapters, see what subplot elements might fit into them. Identify your 'theme' to help decide what kind of minor stories and events you're going to add.

Planning chapters

We've seen that every chapter should include a 'prop', but there are tricks for using the breaks between them to drive the plot along. Plan your chapter breaks with care.

Focus point

Chapter breaks are part of the planning of a crime novel, not just spaces where nothing is happening.

- Use them to account for passing time. If there is likely to be an awkward wait, or a lengthy search, end a chapter just as that begins. Make the chapter break become the pause. You can begin the next chapter along the lines of 'Many beers later, the results came through.'
- Use them for changes of location, too. Get into a train at the end of Chapter 1: be at the destination at the start of chapter 2 – it feels like continuous narration. You do not have to account for every hour of time.
- This can be a way of hiding clues (something has happened in the train that we didn't see – but which we could have deduced if we were paying attention: she got on with three bags but got off with two).
- Introduce a new character as a chapter ends. Have them walk in before the break, then describe them after it. This keeps the reader slightly in suspense – which in turn speeds up the narrative.
- End a chapter on a question or a problem to be solved. This is the place to put your second corpse, or the moment when danger suddenly appears, or the silky threatening voice comes on the phone. Don't write the whole scene before the break. Stop at the moment of greatest impact. Think 'cliffhangers', which is the same idea. You want to keep your reader longing to read on. In the following chapter, say what happened next. Write it as if there hadn't been a pause.
- Having a cliffhanger moment is a useful way to avoid the 'mini block' that often afflicts writers every time they stop. If you end a chapter knowing how the next one will begin, it's usually easier to carry on when you come back to it.
- Change the viewpoint character (if you do) at a chapter break. That not only helps with tension, it can keep up the pace, since that probably necessitates a slightly different style – as we'll see in the next chapter.

Write now

Try that last technique. Establish a scene between two characters (use the ones that you've been working on) and write the last few paragraphs before the interruption of the newcomer, which should come as a surprise and be another member of the cast. If you need more guidance, go back to the wall, and have your sleuth interrupted by another 'suspect' character while talking to someone and examining the corpse. But if you have your own ideas by now, that's better still. Then open a new chapter with that character involved. Use the techniques we've looked at to establish them.

Aim for at least a page or so, on each side of the 'break', but continue with the scene if more occurs to you.

Edit exercise

Look at your plot outline again:

- Are there now sufficient 'props' (including those in the subplots) to keep up the narrative?
- Which character's viewpoint do you propose to use for major happenings?
- Are there any long periods of time, or lengthy journeys that can be handled by a chapter break?
- Can the moments for chapter openings and closings be improved?

Make any improvements that you feel would help.

Where to next?

We've mentioned 'viewpoint' characters several times now. In Chapter 6 we shall look at handling viewpoint in more detail, and see how the various methods relate to writing style. We'll have a glance at other factors which affect that, too.

6

Style and viewpoint

In this chapter we look at the various types of viewpoint used in fiction (usually either first-person or third-person narrative) and how this relates closely to style – which should reflect how different characters speak and think. We will also learn that the general dictum 'less is more' applies especially to crime fiction – adjectives and adverbs, metaphors and similes, should be used sparingly so as to intensify their impact when they are used.

Viewpoint and style are closely interlinked

We've briefly mentioned viewpoint characters before. Now we are going to look at how they affect style.

Style matters. The very opening paragraphs give instant clues as to the kind of book that follows. One of the first indications as to whether this novel is a 'cosy' or a 'noir' is the style of writing in those paragraphs, and what viewpoint we first meet.

Workshop exercise

Here is a series of openings from several different genres. Read them and decide what type of book each is. Familiar names and surnames have been deliberately suppressed, so that you only have the evidence of the style.

A

> The girl screamed, only the once.
>
> Even that was a minor slip on his part. That might have been the end of everything, almost before it had begun. Neighbours inquisitive, the police called in. No, that would not do at all. Next time he would tie the gag a little tighter ...

B

> What was your approximate speed when the accident occurred?
>
> That was easy enough: 15mph. Bulldozers don't do more than 15mph flat out.
>
> Position of other vehicle(s) involved. Use sketch plan if necessary.
>
> Bang in front of me side-on to start with. Through 90 degrees and up on its side after I hit it.
>
> Speed of other vehicle(s) involved.
>
> Nil. After I'd hit it, though, I nudged it sideways for a bit with the bulldozer.

C

> 'That's torn it,' said X.
>
> The car lay helpless and ridiculous, her nose deep in the ditch, her back wheels cocked absurdly up on the bank,

as if she were doing her best to bolt to earth and were scraping herself a burrow beneath the drifted snow. Peering through a flurry of driving flakes, X saw how the accident had come about. The narrow hump-backed bridge, blind as a one-eyed beggar, spanned the dark drain at right-angles, dropping plumb down upon the narrow road that crossed the dyke.

D

This is a story of a woman and a city. I saw the city first, glimpsing it from afar as it shimmered like the new Jerusalem in the light of the setting sun. I smelled the sweetness of the land and sensed the nearness of green, growing things after the weeks on the barren ocean. We had just passed through the narrows between Long and Staten Island and were coming into Upper New York Bay. It was Sunday, 2nd August, 1778.

The following morning Mr Noak and I came up on deck...

1 Which of these (there may be more than one – and the same passage may appear in more than one answer) promises to be:

a exciting?

b noir?

c cosy?

d funny?

e intriguing?

2 Which is set:

a in the 1930s?

b earlier than that?

c most recently?

3 What do you notice about the language in each case? (Think back to the chapter about register.) Which passage uses 'officialese' to contrast with the 'proper' narrator?

4 From whose point of view do we see each passage?

a the author's

b a character's

c an invisible bystander's

5 Why do you think so, in each case?

6 Are there any moments when we 'hear' somebody think? What do we already know about these characters?

Key idea

Style matters. It sets the tenor of the book from the first sentence.

Of course, you are the author and all styles and 'viewpoints' will be yours, but – as you can see from the workshop exercise – part of the writer's job is to adapt the style to match the viewpoint of the 'narrator'. (In case you did not spot it, the character in passage C identifies period and shows their education – first by using 1930s' idiom in speech and then carefully thinking 'as if she were' not 'as if she was'. Passage D creates an eighteenth-century narrator by giving them a slightly formal style of thought (poetic similes and longish sentences). All four books and authors are identified in the Answers at the back of the book – together with dates of publication. Are they what you thought?)

In the same way your style should show how different people think. Your characters will all have different outlooks and speech patterns and notice different things. They may have educated confidence, or informal chatty ease – a prevailing 'register', in fact (if you haven't read the chapter about dialogue, you may need to do so now). The style you choose depends on whose the viewpoint is.

So what is 'viewpoint' exactly?

The most common kinds of 'viewpoint' in a narrative

You may have heard of 'first person' or 'third person' narrative and wondered what it meant. The terms derive from learning other languages, especially Latin. When you learn a foreign language there's a pattern to the way you learn the verbs, as you'll know if you have ever studied one (e.g. *je suis*, *tu es*, *il est* – I am, you are, he is, etc.). So 'I' is the 'first person', and 'he' or 'she' becomes the 'third' person. (Apologies if this is all familiar to you.) But what has this to do with viewpoint characters?

FIRST-PERSON VIEWPOINT

In grammatical terms, the first person is 'I'. So a first-person narrator is a character, possibly the sleuth, who purports to tell the story directly, calling themselves 'I'.

This technique is often discouraged in general fiction but it does have real advantages for crime. If the narrator is the sleuth, the reader cannot know things that they do not know, nor see things that they didn't notice at the time! Also, if the character is a sympathetic one, it helps to make the reader empathize with the story from the start.

The 'I' character does not have to be the sleuth. Christie, for instance, has at different times used victims, onlookers and even murderers as first-person narrators, and of course the faithful sidekick, Hastings, narrates the Poirot books.

This is not quite the same as 'internal monologue', as sometimes found in other genres. In crime stories the character is not talking to him/herself but (theoretically) directly to the reader.

A reminder. Personal description of the 'I' character is not needed, unless it is important to the plot. So don't spend time inventing ways to make self-description appear plausible. Get age, name, race and nationality established quickly, and let it go at that. Deeds, thoughts and words including the narrative will establish character. Your readers will be quite content to invent their own mental picture of the narrator.

Focus point

If you are writing first-person narration, you must use the idiom, structure and vocabulary that fits your character.

Snapshot exercise

Here is the opening of *The Hound of the Baskervilles* by Arthur Conan Doyle.

> Mr Sherlock Holmes, who was usually very late in the mornings, save upon those not infrequent occasions when he stayed up all night, was seated at the breakfast table. I stood upon the hearth-mat and picked up the stick which our visitor had left behind him the night before. It was a fine, thick piece of wook, bulbous-headed, of the sort which is known as a 'Penang lawyer'. Just under the head was a broad silver band, nearly an inch across. 'To James Mortimer MRCS, from his friends of the C.C.H.' was engraved upon it, with the date '1884'. It was just such a stick as the old-fashioned family practitioner used to carry – dignified, solid and reassuring.
>
> 'Well, Watson, what do you make of it?'
>
> Holmes was sitting with his back to me, and I had given him no sign of my occupation.

> 'How did you know what I was doing? I believe you have eyes in the back of your head.'
>
> 'I have, at least, a well-polished, silver-plated coffee-pot in front of me,' said he.
>
> Rewrite this scene from Holmes's point of view. See whether you can capture a different 'voice' for him. Change anything around in the narrative you wish. You will have to start in a different place, and project a different attitude to the whole event. Which bits of information will you have to omit, if any? Why do you think the author chose the Watson view?

THIRD-PERSON VIEWPOINT

In this, the viewpoint character is described as 'he' or 'she' (the 'third person' in grammatical terms). This makes it seem at first as if we're not inside their mind, but in fact we still see things from that character's point of view and are party to their thoughts. That's why it's called a 'viewpoint'.

One way of writing this effectively is to write the first draft of any scene as 'I' and change it later on. That way you don't make mistakes about what your viewpoint character should know, what they've done, what they would think and do, or what sort of things they'd say to other characters.

If you are using a third-person viewpoint character, you will still need to capture something of the voice and attitude, while adopting the appearance of normal neutral prose. This means that grammar will be more correct than in first-person narrative, but you can still use short sentences that do not have a verb and other devices of 'informal' register. Look back at the examples we've been examining.

Full physical description isn't needed here either, though a little more is required than for a first-person narrator. The author can drop a few descriptive details here and there, as long as they don't interrupt the flow.

The third-person viewpoint can be anyone except the corpse. But it must be somebody who knows all the facts, or gets to know them in the story. That's virtually a job description for the sleuth, of course, and very often that's the viewpoint character. The sidekick is another useful choice. Always a little less intelligent, the sidekick may reasonably miss things that the sleuth would spot, be mystified by hints, or glide over them in the narrative without alerting us to their significance.

MULTIPLE VIEWPOINTS

It is possible to have multiple viewpoints, viewing events through different people's eyes at different times. However, don't have too many viewpoint characters. Two or three in each novel is generally enough, and only ever have one for any given scene.

> ## Key idea
>
> Only have one viewpoint for a given scene.

There are advantages to the multiple viewpoint technique:

- Different viewpoints are a must where the central characters are in different places at the same moment in the narrative, and the author wants to show the reader both of them. This is why thrillers use this trick a lot.
- In a thriller there are usually two viewpoints as a minimum – the threatener and the victim – and if there is a separate 'rescuer', that character will probably need viewpoint scenes as well.
- One of the viewpoints can be a 'first-person' narrator. This works well for the villain in a thriller. We can share their disturbed delusions as they watch their intended victim's every move.
- You can have one 'viewpoint character' comment on another, giving a description, a history or a view of character.
- Different viewpoints may pick up different details, or give a differing slant on people or events.
- The viewpoint narrator can't lie while we are following their thoughts. They can tell lies in dialogue to another character but they know they are doing that and what emotion prompted it, and therefore so must we. But the author can withhold specific history. For example, we learn that the teacher is feeling guilty and confused and this is somehow connected to the missing girl – but he can refuse to think about the reasons why.
- Changing 'viewpoints' lets the author move between two characters. This is a good way of hiding clues. One viewpoint character knows something, perhaps about an upcoming event, an object or a person's history, that the author isn't ready to disclose. The next narrator does not know it, so – without cheating – a move to that viewpoint means it won't arise.

The victim in a whodunnit may be one viewpoint character, until the moment of the homicide. Of course, the killer must remain a mystery so the narrator mustn't see the attacker in time to register the thought. This is often managed by 'Oh, it's you', or something similar, before the fatal blow, followed by an instant change of scene and viewpoint, naturally. This device is often used in opening scenes.

All this does, however, call for some technique in ensuring that each viewpoint is distinct, using different types of language – idiom, syntax and vocabulary – in line with differing personalities.

One easy trick for doing this is to give your viewpoints different mental strategies. (Refer back to Chapter 2 on settings to refresh your memory.) Let one tell the story with visual imagery, another notice sounds, while a third stresses tactile sensations and smells, or be good with comparisons, sizes, times and dates. The reader won't necessarily notice, but the difference will be there.

Too much mathematical precision appears either sinister or boring, so use that one with care – but keep it up your sleeve, for characters you don't want your readers to like.

Whichever kind of viewpoint you select, the common trick of making a viewpoint character worry afterwards that they have 'missed something' is a useful way of creating tension. The reader will start wondering what they've missed themselves. But make sure that there really was a clue that wasn't emphasized.

George R.R. Martin

'When I'm writing from a character's viewpoint, in essence I become that character; I share their thoughts, I see the world through their eyes and try to feel everything they feel.'

THE EYE-OF-GOD VIEWPOINT

This is where the narrator is not a character at all. It's the all-knowing author, here described as 'god'. This viewpoint can see everything, from every person's point of view in turn, and knows what everybody feels and thinks.

This point of view is not in general suitable for crime. 'God' knows exactly who did it from the start, but can't tell us what the murderer thinks and does. Withholding information contravenes the conventions of the genre.

Also, with no particular human sympathy for any one character, it's hard to empathize. The 'eye-of-god' can make the narrative seem dispassionate and cold.

However, this can be used occasionally to great effect at the right moment in the narrative. This is usually at the start, before the viewpoint character arrives. Even first-person narratives make use of this device, often in a separate prologue detailing the crime.

Experiment with this effect for horror openings. No adjectives and no emotions, please – just cold unpleasant facts. Any attempt to write feelingly diminishes the impact.

> ## Snapshot exercise
>
> Write a paragraph, for your eyes only, describing the most horrendous grisly murder scene you can imagine. Don't spare the adjectives, write it with all the emotion you can bring to bear, as if you've walked in on the scene. Then take the emotion out of it. Become the eye-of-god, retreat to the ceiling and simply state the facts. Use numbers and measurements instead of adjectives. Feel the difference in the two techniques.

Authors may seek this cold detachment as a deliberate device within the narrative, for instance in the form of an extract from a newspaper – a type of writing which naturally uses the 'eye-of-god' technique. Patricia Cornwell does the same thing brilliantly with forensic reports.

Despite what you might think from a cursory glance, modern crime stories are almost always told from the standpoint of one or more of the cast of characters. Even early exponents of the genre, such as Christie and Conan Doyle, used sidekick narrators instead of eye-of-god, which has come to seem extremely dated now.

THE INVISIBLE BYSTANDER VIEWPOINT

There is a final kind of viewpoint we should mention here, sometimes called the 'invisible bystander'. This is rather like the eye-of-god, except that it deals only with appearance and events, not with the thoughts and feelings of the characters.

The bystander only can see what's happening; they cannot know what anybody thinks or what their motives are. This makes the viewpoint, like the eye-of-god, not generally suitable for in a crime novel where feelings, thoughts and motives are the driving force.

This 'bystander' device can be useful for a paragraph or two, before the viewpoint character arrives. Use it to give a description of the scene that your character is just about to walk into (in a locked-room mystery, for instance). Or use it for a brief factual account of an event, for example in a prologue to a historical mystery.

Either way, don't let the invisible bystander take centre stage for long. The real story starts when the character arrives.

WHY IS THERE NO SECOND-PERSON VIEWPOINT MENTIONED HERE?

The second person grammatically is 'you'. This means the reader in a mystery. Making the reader a character – let alone a viewpoint one – is very hard to do. It has been tried, as a technical literary exercise, by writing letters outlining what 'you' have done. Interesting, and very difficult, but not applicable to crime.

Focus point

Your choice of viewpoint will affect the style.

Write now

Rewrite the story of Red Riding Hood (see Chapter 5), but make the wolf your third-person viewpoint character. Begin with 'He was hungry...' or something similar. If you want to experiment with a second viewpoint, you can see where the plot makes that necessary – always a good place to make the change. Alternatively, you can alter the end of the story if you wish. You can make the tale as noir or comic as you like.

Remember that, once you look at things from the wolf's point of view, eating other creatures is not just acceptable – it's what wolves have to do.

Using style to pace the narrative

As well as fitting the viewpoint character, your writing style has other jobs to do:

- Matching the pace of action. Swift action needs short paragraphs, short words, short sentences – unless you are writing about a deviant, in which case the opposite can be extremely creepy. To keep the pace up, make the writing crisp.

- Don't tell the reader what is happening in pieces of intervening narrative. Let the characters do it in action.

Mark Twain

'Don't say the old lady screamed. Bring her on and let her scream.'

- Don't make your sentences too long. Remembering that your viewpoint is a character will help. People don't speak or think in complex sentences – they only write with them, unless they are pedants, in which case do your worst – but don't keep that viewpoint going for very long. You'll bore your readers and they'll put down the book.

Write now

Write an action scene based on the plot that you are working on, or one of the subplots if that's more suitable. Make it violent, if that fits your plan, or at least involve fast movement and physical exertion, or a high degree of risk. A barely averted car crash will do the trick, if your characters don't run. If you didn't have any scene of this description in your plan, it's probably a good idea to plan one now. Aim to put it somewhere part way through, giving you a prop. Bear in mind the short sentences technique and try to make the passage as exciting as you can.

- One line of dialogue can break up a wodge of prose, visually and mentally. Here's a paradox. Adding that line of dialogue can make a static scene seem shorter. Faster too, though there are now more words in it.

Using rhythm, even though you're writing prose

Rhythm is an underrated element of style. Odd, because it shouldn't matter when this is written prose, but everybody mentally 'hears' what they are reading. If your style is cumbersome, it slows the process down. If it is too constantly staccato, it feels frenetic as you read. There's only one way I know of for combating this.

Key idea

Read your work aloud.

It doesn't matter if your housemates think you're mad, it's part of the job. You're listening for the rhythm, which can work for you – or against you if you get it wrong. There's a technical reason why that should be so.

- English is unusual. Unlike most languages, where the rhythm depends on the number of syllables, English is stress-timed. Not all syllables carry the same weight, and when we speak we squash the unstressed ones together and the rhythm is dictated by the ones we stress. Try saying 'I love fish', and 'It's a beautiful day'. One has twice as many syllables as the other, but they both have three stresses – and take about the same time to say. Get two friends to try it, if you doubt. This is why English is so difficult for foreigners to speak – they can't bring themselves to suppress the syllables – and why English is so good for poetry. It's a real effect. So make it work for you. Read your work aloud and listen to the stress.

- If your dialogue sounds awkward while you're reading it, or your connecting narrative is difficult to say, the chances are that you've got the rhythm wrong – too many long words, or too many complicated clauses, which mean that you lose track of the basic sentence stress. Once you know what's causing it, you can put it right. Remember, people hear the words they're reading in their heads, and you'll slow down the narrative if they stumble over stress.

- When you get good at this, you can use it to distinguish different characters. Give one person a slightly different rhythm in their speech (or in their viewpoint narration) and the reader will subconsciously pick up the beat, and know who's speaking without you saying so. It needs a lot of practice before this comes naturally, but it's a useful technique once you master it.

- You've probably been told to avoid repeating words, but in crime writing there are exceptions to this rule. In moments of real tension try this little trick. Echo the human heartbeat by deliberately repeating words or phrases – preferably short ones, with single syllables – with punctuation pauses in-between. (Commas or full stops are 'pauses written down'.) It will affect your readers, without them knowing why. But don't do this more than once in a book. Keep it for the key scene. It's very powerful. Don't even do it in the next book that you write, or your readers may start to notice, which will ruin the effect.

- Don't be afraid of single-word sentences, whatever your grammar teacher said. Miss out the padding words and write action and terror as sparely as you can.

All these techniques are worth acquiring, if you can. But nobody but you should know you're using them.

Key idea

Style is a tool – it shouldn't overwhelm the narrative.

Snapshot exercise

Look at the following extract from the middle of a book.

Creak. She sat up in bed. What was that? She listened. Silence. She was being silly. He couldn't have found her, could he? Not out here. She forced herself to breathe.

Creak. There it was again. Creak. A floorboard. Someone was in the porch. It couldn't be. The gate was locked and the alarm was on. She slid out of bed, crept to the window, and lifted the corner of the curtain cautiously. Nothing. No-one in the porch. The yard and the decking lay silent in the snow.

Brenda Lacey, *Die Easy, Darling*

Try writing a short paragraph to follow this, in which – as in the story – the intruder succeeds in getting in and holding her at gunpoint. Don't forget whose viewpoint we are with.

Making adverbs and adjectives really work for you

If you're working through this book in order, you've already looked at these in the chapters on setting and on dialogue. But the message is so important that it's worth repeating it. Descriptive adjectives – words that tell you what a thing is like – and adverbs of manner – words that tell you how an action was done – are priceless tools but only if you use them sparingly. Make them work for you.

ADJECTIVES

- Don't use many. Pick the ones that really matter. If you're describing something that everyone will know, such as a modern underground station, don't waste your time with 'dirty', 'crowded' and that sort of thing. An unexpected detail will do the trick better, for example a ticket trodden in the dust.

- The opposite is true when you're disguising clues. If you want to hide a red book as a clue, don't just have one colour in the paragraph – and call that book 'maroon' or something when you mention it.

- You can choose one strong adjective for a walk-on character, and stick to it the next time they appear. The more striking the adjective the better. But even 'the surly man' will do the trick.

ADVERBS

The precepts governing adjectives apply here, but even more so.

Snapshot exercise

1   Here are five single lines of dialogue. Add an 'ly' adverb every time to show how it was said.

- 'I love you,' he said…
- 'I'm going to kill you,' he said…
- 'You're an ugly bitch,' she said…
- 'This knife is pointed at your heart,' he said…
- 'I've had enough!' she said…

2   Now apply the adverbs to the other pieces of dialogue instead. What is the effect? What general precept do you derive from this?

3   Here are three adverbs. On which line of dialogue would each have most effect?

a   conversationally
b   regretfully
c   wearily?

Save 'ly' adverbs for when they are unexpected, especially in speech directions. '"I love you," he said tenderly' is almost tautological. If he said it 'dangerously', then it's worth saying so, because that's not the mood the reader naturally supposes.

When writing action, look closely at your 'ly' adverbs. Often they can be omitted altogether, or replaced by using a stronger verb.

See whether 'She went quickly to the door' could be 'She hurried to the door' – it can't always. If the woman here is graceful and composed, 'hurried' doesn't do it. And I've only ever found a way of replacing 'suddenly' and that's with another adverb such as 'abruptly', 'unexpectedly' and the like.

Edit exercise

Look at the action scene you wrote earlier in this chapter. Are there any 'ly' adverbs in it? Can they be replaced? Omitted? What is the result? Can you speed the action by using any of the stylistic techniques we have been looking at?

- Words like 'quite', 'fairly' and 'rather', when used to modify an adjective, take away precision from the prose so save them for the moments when they pack a punch. Don't write 'It was rather chilly in the street by this time', at least not in connecting narrative. (Your characters may say this in dialogue, of course.) If you write 'This account was fairly true', you've made the adverb really work for you by suggesting that it was also partly false.
- Be especially careful of 'quite'. It has two opposite meanings, depending on the kind of adjective that you attach it to. For example, 'He was quite dead' does not mean he was partly dead. If you want a grammatical rule of thumb, it's this: when the adjective has obvious degrees like 'big' or 'long' or even 'pretty', then 'quite' suggests 'a bit' or 'fairly'. If the adjective is absolute, that is, there are no gradations in it – you either are, or you are not – like 'perfect', 'frozen' or 'finished', then 'quite' means 'absolutely' or 'completely'. A quick check for absolute adjectives is that you can't put 'very' in front of them; you can't be 'very perfect'. But there are moments when either sense is possible, for example 'The pages were quite yellow.'
- 'Very' is another adverb that's often overused. It's just a strengthener. Use it only when you mean it.

Mark Twain

'Substitute "damn" every time you're inclined to write "very"; your editor will delete it and the writing will be just as it should be.'

What to cut out to improve your style

Key idea

Final reminder in case you skipped the section on dialogue. Avoid fancy verbs in writing speech directions.

'SAID' IS AN INVISIBLE WORD

- Don't write 'grunted', 'hissed', etc. instead. You wouldn't try to cut out the word 'the'. Treat 'said' in the same way. Save those other speech directions for important moments.
- If you get dialogue right, it will be clear who's speaking anyway and you can miss out the speaker for several paragraphs.
- Or have them do something, instead of giving a speech tag. For example, '"Hello!" Mark popped his head around the corner.'
- Adverbs may be needed when you're writing dialogue, but only if it is
  - important and
  - unclear from the text how the speaker uttered the words.

Focus point

Less is often more in writing crime. Shorter sentences and fewer adverbs and adjectives make for tighter prose. Don't tell the reader what to think.

Mason Cooley

'To understand a literary style, consider what it omits.'

ASSASSINATING CLICHÉ

Try to avoid the very hackneyed phrase. If you have a boring character let them speak in clichés. Don't do it otherwise. Find your own way of saying what you mean. The first person who described something as being 'white as snow' or 'white as a sheet' created a strong image. Do the same yourself: find something in your imaginary world that is especially white and use that to make a simile: 'white as a choirboy's surplice', 'white as a virgin's panties', 'white as a newly sheared lamb', whatever suits your setting.

MURDERING YOUR DARLINGS

And last, but not least, a piece of advice so important that writers from Stephen King to William Faulkner have echoed it:

Arthur Quiller-Couch

'Whenever you feel an impulse to perpetrate a piece of exceptionally fine writing, obey it – wholeheartedly – and delete it before sending your manuscript to press. Murder your darlings.'

Don't be clever or fancy for the sake of it. The style serves the story, not the other way about.

Matthew Arnold

'Have something to say, and say it as clearly as you can. That is the only secret of style.'

Where to next?

We've seen, for instance in the use of adjectives, that stylistic devices can be used to hide a clue. If a character appears to talk in way that seems forced or uncharacteristic, this may be a deliberate hint that something is amiss. In Chapter 7 we'll look again at the whole field of clues – how to invent them, and ways of hiding them.

7

Give us a clue

Clues are, of course, intrinsic to crime fiction, even to so-called 'clueless mysteries'. All the same setting them can be a daunting task even to the most experienced of writers, let alone the first-time ones. This chapter will give you advice about the different types of clue and about how and when to drop your clues into the narrative, without drawing too much attention to them. As you will discover, this is curiously similar to mastering a conjuring trick!

Clues are the defining element of crime novels

All crime novels depend on clues – even the ones described as 'clueless mysteries'. There are several kinds of these.

OPERATIONALLY 'CLUELESS' MYSTERIES

Some of the earliest crime novels from the nineteenth century are described as 'clueless' now. This does not mean that there are no clues – there are often many – but only clues that the reader does not know about until the detective reveals them at the end. Action comics, TV, film and video games still use this kind of plot, and may even boast of it:

 ## T-Rex, Dinosaur Comics

'My detective doesn't show all the clues to the reader! He's always detecting stuff that the reader doesn't know and can't know, and at the end when he figures out the mystery, he arrests the murderer for reasons that we aren't privy to and that no careful reading of the text will ever reveal.'

But don't try writing this kind of plot yourself. Books are different nowadays. Readers – and therefore publishers – expect that the author will 'play fair' and make all clues available to them as they arise. A library survey from 2011 shows that of 200 mystery readers, 98 per cent are disappointed if the author 'cheats' and 87 per cent would never pick up another of their works. And the latest 'Clueless Mystery' website warns against it even for television scripts.

A 'CLUELESS SIDEKICK' AS FIRST-PERSON NARRATOR

This is a modification of the above, which gives the writer a notional alibi – the sidekick cannot tell us what they do not know. Even Sherlock Holmes – who has become a by-word for the use of clues – does not always tell Watson what he's noticed until the solution of the crime, so a reader could not possibly have worked it out. This is slightly more acceptable but rather dated now. Modern readers do not fall for it, as this web review makes clear.

Jim Loy

'*Compare any Agatha Christie story with Sherlock Holmes, and see who cheats. The Sherlock Holmes stories, as great as they are, are almost all unsolvable by the reader. Holmes always hides many of the clues. Agatha Christie gives us all of the clues.*'

MISSED CLUES MYSTERIES

There is a recent 'realistic' trend towards another 'clueless' form, but in these stories there are clues – it's just that the detective didn't spot them at the time. The detective is 'clueless', if anybody is. The perceptive reader may notice what the sleuth did not, or only learn the significance when the sleuth – eventually – works it out, but either way the clue was always there. The idea is that the reader isn't distanced by an all-knowing sleuth, but follows a fallible, muddle-headed one, usually in a police procedural or crime comedy. If you feel you can do this and know enough about procedure to be credible, it's a current trend.

Anjanette Delgado in an online review of 'clueless detective' crime

'*... In an era in which we're no longer sure of anything ... there's something to be said for stories about hero sleuths who don't know it all, but will do what it takes to learn. And so the protagonists in [some] modern detective procedurals have none of the self-assuredness of C. Auguste Dupin, Sherlock Holmes, Jane Marple or Hercule Poirot. Sure, they have lots to learn. But since we do, too, it's nice that they make a point of taking us along for the ride one lesson at a time.*'

THE CLUELESS 'PERFECT' CRIME

Some plots are classified as clueless because the criminal has taken pains not to have left any. That can't be quite the case, of course; otherwise there would be no story. There are clues and the investigating character will find them in the end, although they may be miniscule forensic ones.

Focus point

Dealing with clues is pivotal to any version of the genre.

Workshop exercise

Here is the opening of a prize-winning novel. It uses a number of techniques that you should recognize.

Southern Evening Herald – 23rd March.

GROWING POLICE ANXIETY

Following intensive questioning at airports, docks and ferry terminals in the search for the missing businessman, David Maybury, police have expressed concern for his welfare.

'It's now ten days since he vanished,' said Inspector Walsh, the detective in charge of the investigation, 'and we cannot rule out the possibility of foul play.' Police efforts are being concentrated on a thorough search of Streech Grange Estate and the surrounding farmland.

There have been numerous reported sightings of the missing man over the past week, but none that could be substantiated. David Maybury, 44, was wearing a charcoal-grey pinstripe suit on the night he vanished. He is 5'10" tall, of average build with dark hair and eyes.

Minette Walters, *The Ice House*

How many potential clues can you find in this account? Try writing this opening again, beginning with the discovery of the corpse. What clues would there be to his identity? If you started here, how much back information would you now have to provide? (Think about setting, the time and date of disappearance and the profession and description of the corpse.) Why do you think the author has chosen a newspaper report to start the narrative? What other specialist techniques can you identify?

Snapshot exercise

Take the plot outline that you wrote earlier and make a list of clues which you could introduce. Aim for ten or twelve potential clues – you don't have to use them all; the idea is to create a repertoire.

What clues do and why they are important to your crime novel

Clues are the backbone of most mysteries. The sleuth must follow up such leads and inferences as they have, and sort out the ones that have no relevance. This is most of the business of the book, and the steps they take provide direction for your narrative. If you include 'suspended clues' – those which can't be fully analysed at the time – you have a built-in element of suspense.

Even in crime thrillers you will need to plant some clues. The threat cannot be overcome, or the victim rescued, purely by chance. Working out the clues provides the intellectual 'effort' for the plot, though this must be followed by physical effort, too. Often the clues in thrillers are not concrete ones, but based on perceptions rather than on objects, which often lead the 'good guys' to identify a place. Faint background noises picked up on the phone when the abductor makes the ransom call; a smell that lets the blindfolded victim work out where they are; a flash of bright blue high up on a wall, glimpsed through a cellar window by the prisoner locked inside proves to be a morning-glory plant, which identifies which house it was. These are all real examples of how authors use such clues.

Write now

Select one or more of the clues from your potential list and draft the scene in which the sleuth (or the rescuer or victim, if this a crime thriller) discovers it. Decide what leads this opens up, and see whether you can set up the 'next step' in your plot. Aim to write a page or two at least and incorporate some dialogue in the course of it.

Different types of clue

Not all clues are equal. There are different types which can be combined for differing effects.

All clues give you the sort of unanswered questions we have already recommended for keeping up suspense. If your narrative is sagging, add a few more clues – or end a few chapters with a suspended one.

Key idea

Clues not only help solve the mystery. They are important for keeping up suspense.

OVERT AND OBVIOUS CLUES

If your corpse has a gunshot wound to the head and your sleuth discovers a bullet in a nearby tree, that is obviously a clue and both the detective and the reader realize this. That clue is overt. It does not immediately solve the crime, but gives the narrative direction by suggesting new leads for the sleuth to follow up.

MISSING OBJECT CLUES

Objects don't have to be there to become an overt clue. The fact that your half-buried gunshot corpse has lost one walking boot will almost certainly prompt a search for it – suggesting another direction for the narrative.

SUBTLE AND 'FORESHADOWING' CLUES

These are often the really vital clues, but those which you don't want your reader to recognize. Often they are significant details, the importance of which is not apparent at the time. The implication emerges later in the plot (hence 'foreshadowing') and the clue is recognized only in retrospect. The fact that your murder victim is wearing dark red socks, for example, may be one of these. To play fair with your readers, you must mention it at once, but only in a general description of the corpse – including the colour of everything he is wearing. Some readers will remember the red socks afterwards; others will not notice until you point it out again.

SUSPENDED CLUES

These are clues (alluded to above) that have been openly recognized as potential clues, but to which the answer is not evident at once, and cannot be until some other step takes place. Overt clues are usually suspended ones, especially in these days of modern science. Standard procedure at a murder scene includes a lot of tests, which provides you with a whole range of suspended clues. Go back to that bullet in the tree. The sleuth may, with luck, be able to identify the calibre at the scene, but that is all. A ballistic examination will do far more than that. This hiatus has two effects. First, waiting for results keeps the reader in suspense, giving you the chance to send your sleuth off somewhere. Second, when the answers come they offer further 'leads': who is in possession of a gun like that, and does the bullet 'match' their barrel marks?

Suspended clues may throw up more suspended clues later in the plot. Standard forensic examination at the morgue may discover unexpected fibres on the body which indicate, for instance, that it was carried in the boot of a certain make of car. This clue doesn't surface until the autopsy report.

MISDIRECTION CLUES

Clues may be planted, usually as a deliberate act of misdirection by the criminal. For example, if the forensic tests suggest that the corpse was in a car boot, it's possible that the murderer fired into the tree in order to suggest the murder happened in that wood, when in fact it took place somewhere else. Sometimes the misdirection can be a subtle one: a size-ten footprint doesn't prove there was a size-ten foot! Misdirection clues can add suspense and send the sleuth down dead-end avenues of enquiry – thus delaying the solution of the crime. This can be useful if your resolution is arriving far too fast.

MESSAGE CLUES

Don't overlook the role of messages. Not all are clichés. A victim writing a dying message in blood (which can't identify the murderer, as otherwise there would be no further plot) is such a hackneyed one that it discredits the usefulness of other messages. And no one uses blotting paper nowadays, so don't rely on reading a modern message back to front. There are modern ways of sending messages, apart from the traditional notes and letters. Telephone last-number dial-up facilities, answerphones, tablet computers, texts and emails can all work for you, not necessarily by what the message says, but to identify contacts and narrow down the time of death. Most of these devices record a time and date. Even deleted files can be retrieved, if one of the investigators has the expertise. One of the great advantages of writing is that, if you need such an expert, you can have one. You just write them in.

MISINFORMATION CLUES

Any of the suspects may tell deliberate untruths for reasons of their own, for example offering a spurious alibi to cover the fact that they were having an affair. Note that this is not the same as misdirection, where a false impression is contrived. Here a character tells an outright lie. But it must be a character who lies. It must not be you. Anything written in the author's voice, including first-person narrative, must be trustworthy or the empathy has gone. All misinformation must be disproved before the end, and the motives for the lie revealed. If you are playing fair only the murderer can lie until the last, but people innocent of the crime may lie initially, for other reasons. Misinformation can be the basis for good red herring subplots.

AMBIGUOUS CLUES

These are clues that point to several people, not to only one, or are capable of being read in several ways. If our corpse, when he's identified, proves to be the legal owner of the gun that murdered him, that clue has now become ambiguous. It doesn't identify anyone in particular, but it narrows down the field. It now points us to anyone who knew he had the gun and could get access to it at the time, which may apply to several characters. This type of clue can give direction for the plot by throwing suspicion on a range of characters (though the criminal may offer a misdirection by lying though his teeth) and offering new directions for the sleuth to follow up.

LOGICAL CLUES

Here the clues are not purely physical. Often they're included in a piece of dialogue. For example, a witness mentions that our victim's socks were red, though she says that she only met him in the pub much earlier in the day when our victim was still wearing both his boots. Walking boots are high cut. How does the witness know the socks were red? Or the logic may derive from simple reasoning by the sleuth – this was a murder, not a hapless suicide. The corpse was half buried; it could not inter itself.

🔑 Key idea

Logical clues make the best decisive ones in the solution of the crime.

EXTRACTED CLUES

Hard-boiled and noir crime in particular may include a number of 'extracted' clues. A witness offers information, not by accident or choice, but because someone is threatening to blow their kneecaps off, or break their thumbs and fingers one by one. Crude, compared to intellectual methods of obtaining clues, but gripping and effective all the same. Don't, however, rely entirely on this – there must still be mental effort of some kind as well, although a final confession may be obtained this way.

CLUES THAT SHOULD BE AVAILABLE, BUT AREN'T

It is surprising how often, in a crime novel, the CCTV wasn't working at the time of the crime, or the night-watchman was not at his monitor. Try to eschew such clichés if you can, though sometimes such things are unavoidable. Better to have an unexpected 'glitch' in a firm's security than to make your modern crime scene unbelievable by the lack of any credible security at all. However, if your night-watchman is a party to the crime, or is craftily diverted by the murderer, that, of course, is entirely different.

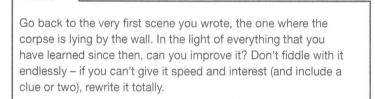

Focus point

Don't rely on one type of clue alone. Use a variety.

Snapshot exercise

Look back on the list of potential clues you made earlier. Into which category does each one fall? Have you got variety, or are they all the same type? Can you improve or widen the list at all?

Using different sorts of clues and spacing them strategically throughout the book will keep your readers – and your protagonist – alert and on their toes. That, after all, is what you're aiming for.

Edit

Go back to the very first scene you wrote, the one where the corpse is lying by the wall. In the light of everything that you have learned since then, can you improve it? Don't fiddle with it endlessly – if you can't give it speed and interest (and include a clue or two), rewrite it totally.

G.K. Chesterton (British Detective Club, oath of membership)

'Do you promise that your detectives shall well and truly detect the crimes presented to them using those wits which it may please you to bestow upon them and not placing reliance on nor making use of Divine Revelation, Feminine Intuition, Mumbo Jumbo, Jiggery-Pokery, Coincidence, or Act of God?'

How and where to hide clues that you're hoping to suppress

Key idea

Think like a conjuror when disguising clues.

The secret to hiding clues is rather similar to learning to become a conjuror. You appear to be doing one thing, while really accomplishing something else which you don't want your audience to see. We have already mentioned several strategies for this:

DISTRACTION STRATEGIES

A conjuror learns to draw the audience's attention to what his right hand is doing – often by his patter – while his left is secretly doing something else. There are similar strategies available to you.

Hide objects among other objects

An important object can be mentioned among a collection of similar or related things, especially in an over-detailed description of a scene. This is the moment to use your adjectives. The reader's tendency to 'skip' will work for you. Don't, however, write a simple list unless it is excused by other aspects of the plot: a police officer making a formal record of the contents of the victim's wallet, for example, where a driving licence would not be remarkable (until we discover that the victim could not drive).

Smother small details in the text

When the clue is not a concrete thing but, for example, the position of the tree, smother that information somewhere, preferably in relation to something different. For example, the sleuth is standing at the corpse's feet and has been bending over to examine them. So he takes off his coat and hangs it on the oak tree behind him. We now know where the tree is relation to the corpse – which may have implications for ballistic evidence.

Use an overt clue to disguise a subtle one

The presence of overt clues in a scene draws attention away from the subtle ones. Mention that your corpse has lost one walking shoe, leaving his right foot covered only in a dark-red sock, and the reader – like the sleuth – will pay much more attention to the absence of the shoe than to the presence of the socks.

Follow a major spoken clue with sudden violent action or an emotional or unexpected scene

This is the classic distraction strategy, but it only really works with spoken clues. For example, if your sleuth discovers an anomalous object just before a violent scene, they will still have it afterwards – not so with dialogue. You are relying on the reader's attention becoming focused on the ensuing scene, so that what was said immediately before slips out of consciousness. The more casual the apparent context of the speech and the stronger the action, the more effective the disguise will be.

SLEIGHT-OF-HAND STRATEGIES

The quickness of the hand deceives the eye as the conjuror hides something important up his sleeve. You can do something like this with words.

Use an uncharacteristic action as a clue

One of your established characters casually does (or appears to do) something which – had we been paying sufficient attention earlier – we would know was not in character. This is most commonly applied to food and drink. For example, a bill for a recent seafood dinner is discovered in his desk, though his mistress has mentioned that shellfish made him ill – hence, he was either lying to her, or it was not his bill at all. The two events must be well separated in the book, and both should seem entirely casual at the time.

Use distraction techniques

She testifies that he had arthritis of the knee, but couldn't take pills with shellfish additives, while the sleuth's reaction to discovering the bill focuses almost entirely on the cost.

In a different context, a tiny action hinting that obsession is afoot, or an indication that no barriers are fixed, can be a first pointer in a psychological crime.

Have one of your cast speak uncharacteristically

This is an altogether more subtle kind of clue and depends upon your ear for dialogue. If the cowed wife of a domineering man suddenly has a lot to say and begins to offer opinions of her own, it's possible that she already knows he's dead. If a phone message comes in a familiar voice, but the words don't fit the character – is the person being forced to make the call? As with behaviour, carefully planted fragments of speech and thought can give the first inkling of a disordered mind.

Have a character know something that they shouldn't logically know

This is a trick best used in dialogue. Somebody says something – preferably throwaway – which either demonstrates (to the alert) that some previous version of events is false, or recounts some detail that only the murderer could know. This works best if no one notices until long afterwards.

Use walk-ons

They can drop pieces of information, innocuous to them, which the alert will notice. 'Should have delivered this earlier but there was a bloody great van outside.'

Have two characters give slightly different versions of events

If they disagree on something major – which can be sorted on the spot – readers often overlook the smaller variations in the rest. The small variations are the crucial ones, of course.

PATTER AND MISDIRECTION

The conjuror's patter leads you to agree to something which is palpably untrue. 'You can see this chest is empty', but, of course, it's not – there are simply mirrors reflecting empty space. All red herrings are misdirection clues. You can also use:

- **characters making genuine mistakes,** telling the sleuth and reader what they honestly believe they saw and heard
- **deliberate misinformation** by the murderer (as above)
- **intentional untruths,** offered to preserve an innocent character's marriage, job or reputation
- **photographs or recordings that are misleading** because they are ambiguous or don't show all the truth. However, don't overdo this one. It works much better on radio or on film where the originals can be experienced by the audience direct, without the need for detailed description, which is all a novel writer can provide. But a cropped photograph, where someone has innocently cut it down to fit a frame, remains a possibility.

Eight traps to avoid when managing your clues

1 Having all your clues arrive at once.
2 Having your detective solve them all at once.
3 Not disguising your clues sufficiently.
4 Hinging a clue on specialist knowledge that your reader does not share.
5 Relying on clues that are too unlikely or too complex to be credible.
6 Planting suspicious things in Chapter 1 and then forgetting them.
7 The trap of using modern electronic clues.
8 The trap of getting your 'real-world' facts awry.

Let's look at these in more detail.

1 HAVING ALL YOUR CLUES ARRIVE AT ONCE

Your crime scene is probably the starting point for your enquiry. Obviously you must establish clues, but it is not a good idea to have too many overt ones at one time. Your readers will not thank you if there is overload. Try to ensure either that:

- There are not many physical clues to be found because the murderer has been careful, OR
- Some clue-gathering is delegated by the sleuth so that you have a reason for not producing all of them at once, OR
- Make most clues into suspended ones, by getting crime-scene officers quickly on the scene – they can report their findings later

in the plot. This frees the sleuth to leave the scene and follow other leads such as visiting the address on the victim's driving licence, all of which combines to keep the pace afloat.

- Have the attendant pathologist refusing to be drawn even on the likely time of death, saying nothing's certain till a proper autopsy. Does that sound familiar? Now you know one reason why it crops up so often.

Limiting the number of overt clues brought in at one time will give you freedom to set up some 'foreshadowing' ones for later use. Suspended ones will give you structure for what happens next.

Write now

You have the basis of an opening scene involving the corpse who lost his walking boot. As a consolidation exercise, write the scene in full, deciding on the following elements.

- Who is the viewpoint character? Is this first- or third-person narration?
- Who is the corpse, and what is it doing there?
- Exactly where is the corpse? How long has the person been dead, and how was it discovered?
- How much description do you need?
- Who else is at the crime scene? Include some dialogue.
- Deal with the overt clues and at least one 'hidden' one.

2 HAVING YOUR DETECTIVE SOLVE ALL YOUR CLUES AT ONCE

This is a good deal more difficult to avoid. The resolution of the mystery requires you or your chosen character to explain. But if you simply work through the logic step by step, pointing out the relevance of every clue in turn, the information quickly becomes indigestible. Whoever is explaining has to talk too much, and too much of anything makes the reader's interest flag. Also, if you think back to our work on dialogue, you'll realize that the tone will be informative, the highest conversation register there is, requiring concentration on the reader's part. This leads to a kind of mental 'overdose' of facts. The easiest solutions are the following:

- **Solve a little of the mystery as you go along.** Don't have all the resolution at the end. Your sleuth (or victim, if you're writing a crime thriller) can make small discoveries from the very start, even if it's just the identity of the corpse, or the presence of traffic noise during a threatening phone call. It helps to have someone they can talk it over with, so the reader is informed at every point.

- **Break down the resolution scene into several smaller ones.** You may even be able to get some real detecting over early in the plot. A popular device is a progress meeting of the investigative team:

So we know who he was, where he was killed and when, and even that he was strangled before that shot was fired – but we're no closer to finding who murdered him and why. Harry, you've been talking to his former wife. Anything of interest to report?

or

Okay, we know that it's a man – the voice analysis suggests he's middle aged. Slight Geordie accent that he's trying to disguise. And he knows this area. But that's all we've got.

- **Break up the final exposition with questions and remarks from other characters.** That does a little to remove the 'wodge' effect. Try not to let one utterance go on for more than half a page, without someone or something interrupting it.
- **Break up the exposition with action if you can.** Do this even if it's only somebody arriving with the final evidence.
- **Don't forget the final little 'grace-note' scene.** If the solution has been long and difficult, you can leave a few of the more trivial clues to be light-heartedly explained during the final wind-down. However, you should never do this with any major clues and never as the central action of the grace-note scene.

3 NOT DISGUISING YOUR CLUES SUFFICIENTLY

We have talked before about how to hide a clue. Nothing reads more badly than a 'leaper' clue, which jumps out of a paragraph. If you want those red socks to be a later clue, then:

- mention more than just the socks – talk about all the clothing on the corpse
- if you are going mention the colour of the socks, write about the colour of the other clothes as well.

If those socks still seem too prominent, make the sentence appear to be chiefly about something else, in this case probably the missing shoe. It's like the conjuror again – you are 'leading' the reader to look past the socks. Of course, you can always try a double-bluff. You can draw attention to the socks as a way of setting up a later clue about the shirt. But you'll irritate your readers if you do this more than once.

Snapshot exercise

Look at the following paragraph. It is clue-heavy. There are four clues in it – the purse, the key, the necklace and the marks around the neck. Can you rewrite it, disguising two of them? Add any other details that will help you in this task.

He looked down at the body of the girl. There were livid fingerprints around the neck – not made by the diamond necklace, which was lying on the floor. In her left hand she still clutched a key, and an open, empty purse was beside her on the bed.

4 HINGING A CLUE ON SPECIALIST KNOWLEDGE THAT YOUR READER DOES NOT SHARE

Don't expect your reader to pick up arcane clues. This is part of the play-fair strategy. If the solution hinges on – let's say – an entry in the victim's diary, 'Friday – cancel TLS', don't assume that your readership will immediately think of the *Times Literary Supplement*. This does not mean that you cannot use this clue at all, but make sure that your characters discuss it openly and thus explain those letters to your readership. Otherwise your sleuth's discovery that these are the initials of a jealous lady-love, and nothing to do with the magazine at all, will be completely lost. This is a rare literary example of the trap, but the same principle applies to all new technologies, technical equipment, arcane food and engineering spares.

5 RELYING ON CLUES THAT ARE TOO UNLIKELY OR TOO COMPLEX TO BE CREDIBLE

A man in a speeding train may glimpse a notice board – it defies belief to tell us that he read the notices. An ingenious device for firing darts, which requires strings and pulleys and a full page of explanation as to how it works, cannot be usefully enlisted as a clue. As a rule, unless you are writing comedy, don't use any clue you don't believe yourself, or couldn't describe to someone on the phone.

6 PLANTING SUSPICIOUS THINGS IN CHAPTER 1 AND THEN FORGETTING THEM

Few things irritate the reader more than clues you planted and then forgot to use. Doing this on purpose, as a sort of tease, merely serves to distract interest from the plot. Remember the principle of 'Chekhov's gun'.

Anton Chekhov

'If you say in the first chapter that there is a rifle hanging on the wall, in the second or third chapter it absolutely must go off. If it's not going to be fired, it shouldn't be hanging there.'

7 THE TRAP OF USING MODERN ELECTRONIC CLUES

Email and answerphones are often used for clues, as are tweets and texted photographs. Using these will make you feel as though you're being up to date, but beware – technology can move on very fast indeed, possibly before you make it into print, and then it may date you just as certainly. This is a reason why people often set their work just a year or two earlier than the current date and also why they write historicals.

8 THE TRAP OF GETTING YOUR 'REAL-WORLD' FACTS AWRY

There are some clues (how soon rigor mortis will set in, for instance) that rely on general facts external to your book. An error here will undermine your plot. Readers see it as 'sloppiness' and don't easily forgive. The greatest danger lies not with what you know, or even with what you know you don't know – but with what you *think* you know. If you intend to use 'external' clues, perhaps by citing forensic evidence, make certain of your facts. Don't wing it – look it up or, better still, find somebody who genuinely knows. This trap is particularly relevant to people writing police procedurals – and to writers of historicals, of course.

Snapshot exercise

Check through your list of potential clues again. Apply this list to them. Do any of them fall into these traps? If so, what modifications could you make?

Focus point

Make sure that you get your real-world information right, especially if you're going to base a clue on it.

Edit exercise

Think of the novel outline that you wrote earlier or use your own intended novel if you have got that far. Have you considered where to place your clues? If so, have you spaced them throughout the plot? If you haven't yet thought about what clues you might include, do so now. Decide on one or two most likely ones. Does that give you any structure or suggest what might happen – what your sleuth will do in the next chapter, for instance, and what other characters you will need to introduce?

Where to next?

We've seen that it's important to be sure about your facts. You can invent almost anything in your fictitious world, but things that derive from the real world must be accurate. Your background detail, your description of a period, your forensic and police procedures – or the lack of them – will be essential to the success of what you write. Put someone on a train from London to Penzance on the afternoon of 14 August 1910 and there will be a reader who could tell you not just what time it left, but how long it took, where it stopped en route, and what kind of locomotive was pulling it. You have two options: check it out or keep the details vague. Either way, you'll need to do enough research to get it right. That is what Chapter 8 is about.

Getting your facts straight

Writers of any fiction may need to do research, but crime writers do most of all. This is because their readers are not reading passively but are alert to discrepancies and aware of details – *because they might be clues*.

The different kinds of general research

There are two main types of general research: background research and spot research. They are different and need to be approached in different ways.

BACKGROUND RESEARCH

This is the kind of research you do before you start. It is exactly what the name implies – research into the background to your narrative. And that does mean your narrative. You don't have to read everything ever written about the National Health Service in order to write a story featuring a nurse. Researching should be interesting and sometimes even fun. Don't make it a burden, or an excuse for never being able to get down to writing.

However, if you have chosen to set your crime novel in a different period, or in another country, you'll need to do some measure of preliminary research unless you are already an expert in the field – and most likely even then.

There may be research connected with your characters as well. Whether your protagonist is a lawyer, a refuse collector or a press photographer, you'll have to have some idea of what such people do, how their day is organized and what kit they will require for the job in order for the crime to take place credibly.

If you're not wholly familiar with the setting and milieu, it's essential to do a modicum of this type of research first – at least enough to get the basic details right. It's best to do it before you start to write at all, but after the first few pages is permissible because you're likely to be revising them in any case. Don't put it off and do it afterwards, or you may discover something which makes the plot impossible.

SPOT RESEARCH

This relates to isolated facts that suddenly crop up and would take two minutes to check up on the Internet. For example, how do you spell the Roman name for Richborough? If you drove due west from Lincoln, Nebraska, what road would you be on? Here exactly the opposite applies. Don't stop the flow of writing to check this sort of thing – just mark it with an X, or dots or brackets or 'TBC' (to be checked) or whatever form suits you. Write down the question on a jotter and check it afterwards. Then, next time you sit down to write, go back and fill in the blank.

Background and spot research apply to any kind of novel. There's another whole field to think of if you are writing crime.

Specialist areas of research

There are some specialist requirements for crime stories. These are generally facts from the real world relevant to death, wounds and weapons, which some readers will inevitably know in detail and even non-specialists may well recognize. Even if they are simply avid readers of the genre, people accumulate surprising amounts of knowledge in this area. If you get your facts wrong here, you will forfeit their belief and with it their interest in your narrative. So, unless you have a background in the police and/or a real familiarity with forensic medicine, it is likely that you will need to engage in some specialist research.

Here are a few examples of things you ought to check:

- The facts on rigor mortis, how soon it sets in and when it dissipates
- The factors (temperature, humidity, air circulation, etc.) that can affect this, either way
- How soon after death a corpse begins to smell – and what it smells like when it does
- How decayed – or otherwise – your corpse should be, given the time of death you have decided on
- What physical results would be produced by the cause of death that you propose
- How much forensic science would be available to your sleuth, what it could work out and to what degree of certainty
- What factors might interfere with such results
- What kind of wound a given weapon makes
- Where a bullet is likely to end up if it is fired as and when you say it was
- The timings of any important journeys, planes or transport links – allowing for both directions where applicable. More than one hopeful murder plot has come unstuck because the intended killer could not have got there – and back – in time.
- How much of a given poison is required to kill a healthy man (or a feeble woman, as appropriate), what the symptoms are and how long death will take. The answers may surprise you.
- Does your poison have a flavour that has to be disguised, or can it be delivered other than by mouth?

These are only a few instances, of course – but you see the principle.

Even for a thriller, there will be facts to check:

- How – and under what circumstances – a phone call can be traced (including cell phones and Internet, where appropriate)
- How long it takes to organize a trace on a call
- Journey times etc. (as above)
- The proposed geography of any real building, town or place involved in an abduction

- The physics of any fetters, gags or other physical restraint – check your facts before you have your hero or heroine escape
- The physical results – if any – of being fettered, tied, gagged or deprived of light, air, food, liquids or medicines for any given period of time
- The physical results of being drugged or knocked unconscious – and how long these are likely to persist
- The details of any gun that you propose to use
- Any technology, especially electronic, vital to the course of the story – how it works, what it can do, and what the very latest version is.

You can think of other examples for yourself.

This time you will need to stop and check things at the time, even if it takes an hour or two and interrupts the flow. Plan your murder, then check to see it works, and what the body would be like by the time it's found. You don't want to waste time writing scenes you'll later have to scrap. But don't wait to get every detail before you start to write – get your imagination started then find out what you need.

It can't be said too often. Ultimately what you want to do is write. Don't make research a substitute for getting on with it.

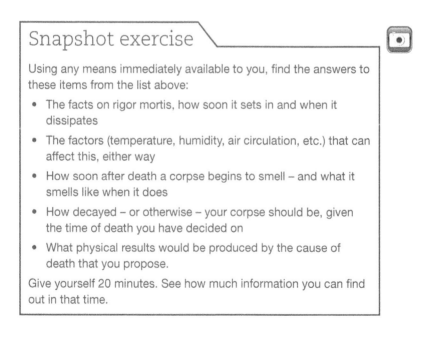

Snapshot exercise

Using any means immediately available to you, find the answers to these items from the list above:

- The facts on rigor mortis, how soon it sets in and when it dissipates
- The factors (temperature, humidity, air circulation, etc.) that can affect this, either way
- How soon after death a corpse begins to smell – and what it smells like when it does
- How decayed – or otherwise – your corpse should be, given the time of death you have decided on
- What physical results would be produced by the cause of death that you propose.

Give yourself 20 minutes. See how much information you can find out in that time.

Edit exercise

Using the information you have just discovered, look at your 'sleuth finds corpse' scene again. Make any amendments necessary to the paragraph. How many were there?

How much is 'enough' research?

It is often tempting to carry on research – especially when it's interesting – to the point where it's a substitute for getting down to writing. Resist this temptation. You're not writing an academic work; you simply want to get sufficient truth in your account to persuade your reader to believe in it.

Key idea

Research is a tool and not an end in itself.

A useful rule (although there are no rules!) is that you need to know about 50 per cent more than the reader needs to know about your imaginary world. Don't get the maths wrong here. You need to know half as much again – not twice as much – so you are only keeping one-third in reserve.

- If you set your plot in a real building on a street, you need to know what lies on either side – though you need not tell the reader, at least not yet. The fact that you have a fuller picture in your mind gives the whole narrative a sense of confidence, and you are unlikely to be tripped up by mistakes. Exactly the same principle applies to any other set of facts that you research.
- When you've told the reader enough for them to visualize the scene and follow what's going on, stop. If you include everything you've been able to find out – be it about a place or a process or what people used to eat – you have written in far 'too much' research. It is very tempting to display your scholarship when you've taken the trouble to research a lot of facts, but make it your target to always keep one-third in reserve. Console yourself by thinking you might need it later on – either elsewhere in the narrative or in the next book that you write.

- If the scene requires that you write down all you know in order for the reader to understand what's happening, that's an indication that you need to find out more. You don't have enough slack to make the story read convincingly.
- Don't put all your research in your story in one lump or even in one chapter. It's like description – too much all at once is indigestible and your reader will skip over it, which will be a waste! Hold a little back and drip-feed it slowly as you go along. You want your reader to assimilate the facts you offer, without being distracted from the narrative.
- Try to keep your information relevant to the action of the plot. If your story is set in another country, and they don't have kitchens as we understand the word, then it is reasonable to have your character go to the 'cooking room' and look about, giving you an opportunity to describe the scene they see. That's all. No interpolated paragraphs about how things are different in East Africa – unless it is your character who is thinking that.
- Don't add facts that are irrelevant, just because you find them interesting yourself.
- Don't let your researched details hold the action up. Weave them in while something else is happening. Seeming discreetly knowledgeable is fine, but lecturing is not.

Carl Hiaasen

'You can do the best research… but if readers don't get past the third paragraph you've wasted your energy and valuable ink.'

Focus point

Research should sit easy. If it shows, you haven't used it well.

- Don't use lists – or any other clue-skimming devices – in paragraphs where you're using your research to give a lively background to your scene. You don't want your readers skipping over this, making your hard work superfluous.
- The easiest way of discovering what additional details you need to know (once you've checked your basic background facts) is just to start to write. When you reach a point when you can't

'see' the scene in your mental eye, because you don't know what would be there, or what – for instance – your sleuth would have to do next, stop. Go and find out what you need to know, and a little extra for good measure, too. Then get back to writing, using what you now know.

David McCullough

'In time I began to understand that it's when you start writing that you really find out what you don't know and need to know.'

Some special requirements

Some subgenres have special requirements, both for research and how to handle it. This is true of police procedurals as well as exotic and historical crime.

POLICE PROCEDURALS AND HOW TO HANDLE THEM

- Find out what proper police procedure is, then use rather less than half of what you know.
- If you applied to the 50-per-cent rule here, and wrote two-thirds of what there is to know about how the police proceed, you would bore your reader stiff with paperwork. Unless that's part of the frustration you're creating for your cop, make it sketchy – have your solver mutter over all the form-filling and don't spend time on it yourself.
- Most successful fictional police are mavericks, so find out how the power structure works. Don't make them too senior or they won't be credible. Don't make them junior either or they will have to do as they are told and cannot operate alone. Of course, if you want tension you can play on that...

GEOGRAPHICAL (EXOTIC) CRIME – INCLUDING THRILLERS AND 'COSIES'

The same is true of places. Some readers actively seek out stories about towns and places they have visited. This is both a blessing and a curse.

Places close to home

- If you have not been there, don't attempt to 'wing it' from a guide book or tourist brochure. Either go and find out what it's like, or set your story somewhere else. Remember the 50-per-cent rule – you must know comfortably more about it than your reader does.
- Don't rely on memory. Places change. Get a recent map and make sure that major buildings and main streets are where you say they are.
- However, you do not have to have experience a dingy nightclub to have some impression of what it might be like – and there does not have to be one where you imply there is. Just don't be too exact with street names and the like.

Exotic locations

All of the above applies – but doubly so, not less:

- If your setting is somewhere like Sri Lanka or Australia, people who have been there will be especially attracted to the book, but are quickly put off by things that don't ring true.
- Films and maps may help with streets, parks and monuments, but there is more to a place than just geography. You need to capture smells and sounds and atmosphere. This is one area where it genuinely helps to 'write what you know'.
- On the same topic, beware of writing something libellous. If you describe an actual restaurant and someone in your story dies of poisoning, you are on tricky ground. This is also a good reason for not recreating the acquaintances you made while you were there.

Geographical settings in the past are a special case, and belong to a discussion about historicals.

HISTORICALS

'The past is a different country', it is said, so all the above criteria apply, but if you are not setting your story in living memory, no reader can know much more about it that you can learn yourself. That doesn't mean that you can make it up. Many readers choose this genre on purpose to experience a different society and time. But there are decisions to be made about how accurate your picture ought to be:

- Physical things must be factually correct. If you have to write a dining scene, try to imagine what is on the table (food, including how and by whom it would be served and cooked, and what kind of lights and implements were used) and if you don't know, find out.

- Social, moral and emotional matters are more difficult. For example, Roman citizens had slaves and did not value women very much, so a Roman man with genuinely Roman views would come across as most unlikeable today. Anyone writing about the period will have to find some kind of compromise between authenticity and reader sympathy. Have a look at the ways that different authors tackle this.

- Speech is another problem. Characters from other centuries, even those who spoke English of a sort, certainly did not speak twenty-first-century English. (How much you portray this is partly up to you. When I discovered there was no exact word for 'yes' in Latin, I took care to never use the word in dialogue again – though I hope it doesn't show!) No one wants to read a faithful transcript of Elizabethan English in a murder story – but having people chat in modern idiom can spoil the mood. It's rather like writing regional dialect: research the language, add a phrase or two when writing dialogue, but keep the touch quite light.

- There may be so many customs and details to explain that it is easier to write a factual forward or a glossary than try to do this unobtrusively in the narrative. Many writers of historical crime do something of the kind. This also gives you the opportunity to say, 'I couldn't find out the facts on so-and-so, so I've just made an educated guess.'

🔑 Key idea

With a historical mystery be as accurate as you can, but try to disguise that this springs from research.

Where to look

There are many sources of information nowadays, many of which have been already mentioned in this text. Some of the most important are:

- **Books and libraries.** This is still your primary resource. There are reference books on almost any topic you can name, biographies can give you insight into other ways of life and other times, and archived newspapers can be a useful source of local information on all sorts of recent things. Learn to use the computer in your library to search for what you need, but don't be afraid to ask your librarian for advice. There is also a useful list in the Appendix to this book.

- **County archives.** In the UK, most counties have a local archive and an archivist. Ask at your library or county hall. There may also be a specialist local library with primary source material accessible for research on the premises (though often not available to take away). Ring up a day or two before you hope to go, tell the librarian what you want to know, explain that you're researching for a book, and relevant material will often be sorted out for you to come and look at on the appointed day. Be prepared to use a microfiche, and bring a soft pencil and a writing pad. Taking photographs of materials is generally prohibited.
- **Photographs, pictures, diagrams and maps.** Sometimes a picture can be worth a thousand words, especially if you are writing about other times and places. If you're writing about a modern city, get a decent street map and a copy of bus timetables and other transport routes. Most tourist offices supply these free of charge. Estate agents' advertisements, and free property papers, can be a useful source of information about an area you want to learn about.
- **Monuments and statues** can be very useful for ancient history. Graveyards and gravestones can give a picture of a village and a useful source of authentic local names. As an example, visit Bath Abbey and look up at the walls – how many of Jane Austen's characters, surnames or forenames, can you find on the inscriptions there?
- **Diaries, letters and memoirs** – if you can find them – are wonderful resources for historicals and stories set abroad. Some of these are obviously available in print, but don't neglect private and family sources as well.
- **Don't overlook museums, art galleries and other exhibitions,** also local churches, factories and stately homes. There are specialist museums (including a police museum) which are excellent and whose curators are generally enthusiasts – extremely helpful and very well informed.
- **Ask living people.** If you are writing police procedurals, it will probably pay you to befriend your local force. Explain what you are doing and ask whether they can help. Make a list of the most pressing things you want to know, and be prepared to go and talk to them – don't expect an answer on the phone. Once they realize that you are serious, the police are often anxious to oblige – though obviously they cannot tell you

everything. I've known crime writers with contacts in the force who have had such valuable advice that it has actually helped them to devise a plot from scratch. However, do not make a nuisance of yourself.

- **Don't be afraid to ask professionals** you know in other fields as well. I've had useful information (including reference books) from a dentist, an ophthalmic surgeon and an undertaker – all of whom were pleased to think that they could help. Be realistic, though. If you're writing about a lawyer and you don't have one as a friend, you may have to consider paying for their time if you want to approach one as part of your research.

 ## Mariska Hartingay

'I did more research than I ever wanted to, and saw some things I wish I didn't. I went on ride-alongs, spent time with… detectives… viewed an autopsy, went to a police firing range and witnessed court cases. And I read, read, read.'

- **Use the Internet.** It is the first thing that most people think of nowadays, anyway. But don't rely on it. There are no editorial or other checks on it. It is only as good as the person posting the information there. If you plan to use a fact found on the Internet, try to verify it from another source before you do, and certainly before you make it central to the plot. University and local history websites are the exception here.

Sherryl Clark

'Don't rely on the Internet for everything. Yes, it's handy and you can find heaps of things there, but it should only be one of your sources… There are many, many websites that are created by people with a specific interest in a subject. That doesn't mean they're expert. I've found many sites with inaccurate information, or pushing a certain point of view.'

- **Read other fiction.** See film and watch TV programmes that deal with setting, periods and subjects similar to yours. Sometimes they'll give you a visual picture that you can't get otherwise. But don't treat these as gospel either. There have been some amazing howlers on screen.

- **Lastly, check up on your assumptions.** It's easy to write about the things you know, and straightforward enough to check on things you don't. The trouble often arises where the author doesn't know that they don't know.

Focus point

Remember that the danger area is what you *think* you know, but have not checked or questioned.

Workshop exercise

Here are four situations from the early versions of real novels, on each of which a portion of the plot depends – and which managed to slip past the editors. The authors' names have been suppressed to avoid embarrassment. What is the matter with these scenarios, if anything?

1 The farmer who sells his other possessions to buy a bullock to build up his herd

2 The motorcyclist who reverses at high speed down the street to get away

3 The garden-loving murderess who arranges a bunch of innocent-looking flowers in a vase for her sick husband, thus smuggling in some monkshood, which she later infuses in his cup of herbal tea

4 The girl who knocks her kidnapper unconscious by dropping a two-pound coin on him from the top window of an empty tower block.

Check your answers at the back of this book and decide what adaptations or amendments (if any) should be made.

Snapshot exercise

1 Make a note of the sources you have used to check facts for the exercises suggested in this chapter. How many different sources did you manage to consult? Did you only use the Internet?

2   Make a list of any additional sources available to you where
    you are:

    a   in that room

    b   in that building

    c   within five or ten minutes from where you're sitting now.

    Don't forget people, text messages and telephones.

4   What specialist sources are available within ten miles? You
    may find the Internet and telephone directory of some help to
    you for this.

5   How many of these have you ever consulted?

What to leave out

- Anything that isn't relevant to the setting, the action, the characters or the plot (see above).
- Any 'interesting' device, historical costume, machine or instrument that requires more than two lines of explanation, unless it is absolutely crucial to the plot. In that case, spread the explanation out – drip-feeding across several paragraphs.
- Dates expressed as figures, distances, dimensions and calculations, again unless essential to the plot.
- More than one example of research per paragraph. If that proves really difficult, reduce your sentence length, and write more paragraphs. Employ a heading if necessary, as an opening.

Snapshot exercise

Here is some information taken from the Web concerning the year 1715 AD. Imagine you were writing a crime novel involving a rich young Englishwoman of the period. Which facts would you use in the first page or two, which would you save for later, and which would you omit?

The woman can be dead or alive, as you decide.

- Easter Day 1715 was 21 April.
- All the bells in London were rung at Easter to call the faithful to church.
- A man could not be a Methodist minister in 1715 unless he fasted on Wednesdays.

- In 1715 the favourite fashion was the *robe à la française*.
- A German-speaking Protestant (George I) was king.
- The Old Pretender lived in exile, and in 1715 he made a last attempt to claim the throne, landing in Scotland and attempting to raise an army there.
- The *robe à la française* (or sack-back gown) with flowing pleats from the shoulders was originally an 'undress' fashion, meaning that it was not worn at court. For formal wear, the front was fitted to the body by means of a tightly laced underbodice, while the back fell in loose box pleats. The gown could be closed in front, or open to reveal a matching or contrasting petticoat. Embroidered stomachers were popular.
- Stays were long-waisted and cut with a narrow back, wide front and shoulder straps; the most fashionable stays pulled the shoulders back until the shoulder blades almost touched. The resulting silhouette, with shoulders thrown back, very erect posture and a high, full bosom, is characteristic of this period and no other. Drawers were not worn at this period.
- In the eighteenth century people could buy paste or paper eggs at Easter time, in which small gifts were hidden and exchanged.
- Richer households could buy water from private companies, but most people drank water from the Thames, which was famous for its stench, since there was no filtration or sanitation of any kind. The city ran on coal and wood.
- Cinder smoke, mingled with the rank odour of the city's decaying garbage, open sewage and decomposing corpses, and the stench emanating from the Thames, created such a powerful stink that, with a proper wind, London could be smelled from several miles away.

Focus point

Don't include information just because it interests you.

As usual, in crime there are exceptions here. If some unusual fact or local custom is a clue, hide it by immediately adding some even more striking or peculiar fact that you've discovered. It's important to write this in as soon as possible – as soon as you can manage it convincingly. You can even draw attention to this second point through an exchange of dialogue. The idea is to focus the reader's interest on the more amazing fact, so that they forget the other detail. This is another good reason for always keeping some of your research in reserve.

Write now

Write the opening two paragraphs of that 1715 book. Try to remember all the skills you've learned. Try to create the era from the start – but don't overload the paragraphs. If you can do this successfully, you have achieved a lot.

Emergency procedures if you can't find out what you need to know about

UPCOMING ELECTRONIC GADGETS

Nothing dates a book as quickly as old technology. Old-fashioned answerphones may feature on TV, but modern offices – and villains and police authorities – move on all the time. This is always a potential difficulty for the crime writer. Obviously you can't predict what will be standard by the time your book has been published. Overcome this by setting your plot at a particular date, specifying a year or two before the one you're writing in. That way you can ensure that your technology is appropriate.

Check it out. You might be surprised how many crime writers use this stratagem.

THE DETAILED GEOGRAPHY OF A TOWN

Invent a street or two, making quite sure that these names don't actually exist. You can do the same thing with buildings, firms or public monuments. It's not a bad idea to do it, anyway, with the addresses of your characters. It's wise to have a general area in mind so you don't have sleazy nightclubs in the poshest bits, or vice versa, but keep directions vague. Get back to lively detail only when you have your character reach an actual place – a well-known major road or shopping street. Use Google for a street view of that area if you haven't seen it for yourself, but remember that the photos may be fairly old.

HISTORICAL FACTS

If you can't find out from any source at all, either leave it out or keep your phrasing vague. 'He was wearing the distinctive costume of an Imperial priest' doesn't do much for the reader's picture of the scene, but it's better than not offering any glimpse at all. But try to avoid this strategy if possible.

GUNS AND WEAPONS

Avoid specific names, calibres and so on, unless you're sure. Make certain that you know the general capability of the sort of device that you are writing about so that you don't have someone commit murder with a gun that wouldn't kill at that range. Then gloss it over, preferably in dialogue. 'You see this gun? You know what it can do?'

ELUSIVE 'SNAPSHOT' FACTS

As a very last resort, you can do as I once did. Once you've exhausted all the other channels, and the greatest expert you can find can't tell you, ask them for an educated guess. I wanted to know the colour of the Servir's robe and could not discover it. I telephoned the best-known specialist in Roman religion. He laughed and said he didn't really know. He'd never asked himself the question. He rang me back next day. 'I still don't know. It wasn't specified in any documents, and all the pictorial evidence is in stone. But,' he added, 'if I don't know, no one else will either. I should make them reddish-purple.' So I did, though I confessed in the forward that this was just surmise.

> ## Key idea
>
> In desperation, 'hint' at what you do not know. Don't try to wing it by making things up.

> ## Edit exercise
>
> In the light of what you know about rigor mortis etc., look at your original body by the wall. What additional information do you have (for instance, about the time of death) based on your description of the corpse? Are there any details you would now like to include?

So, you have your setting, your characters, your plot and you understand a little about pace, dialogue and style. You've done the research. So now it's time to write. And rewrite, probably. And perhaps revise again. But not ad nauseam. There is a time for editing and a time to stop. That will be the subject of Chapter 9.

9

Writing, editing and redrafting

So you've been working through the text and exercises in this book. Now it's time to write. Don't put it off any longer – begin in earnest as soon as you have finished reading this chapter. It doesn't matter if you get it right first time or not. A book is a long product – it may take several years – and a blank page is daunting. That's why there have been writing exercises in this book, which you are at liberty to build on if you choose. If you have your own ideas for a novel in your mind, so much the better. Get started. Write little bits at first, if that makes it easier. A page a day is a complete novel in a year.

E.L. Doctorow

'Planning to write is not writing. Outlining, researching, talking to people about what you're doing, none of that is writing. Writing is writing. Writing is like driving at night in fog. You can only see as far as your headlights, but you can make the whole trip that way.'

Here are a few final hints to help you on your way.

Don't spend too long perfecting your opening chapter or paragraph

This might seem like contradictory advice. We said before that openings are key, because the first few pages are what grab a reader first. That's true. The point is not to worry about getting the opening perfect straight away. For now, it's more important to have something on the page. If you haven't already got an opening that you like, just write something half suitable and get started on the plot. There are several reasons for this:

- You will almost certainly want to change the opening anyway, when you get into your stride. The more you write the more you hone your style – so the later you write your final version the better it will be. If you want the best one possible, acknowledge that your first attempt will only be a draft, then come back to it. It's not uncommon for authors to finalize that first sentence last of all.
- With a crime novel especially, you will find that there are clues and hints that you will think of as you go, and that you may wish to 'write into' the first chapter later on. You won't want

to spoil that perfect opening once you've spent hours on it, so make it provisional for now and give yourself the flexibility to change.

- There's always a temptation to give too much back story to your characters. It's a very common fault, especially with first-time authors. So here's the trick. Once you know you're going to rewrite the opening, you can give yourself permission to include as much back story as you like in your first draft of it (this may help you understand your characters, yourself). Then make a point of cutting it out when you revise and finding some other way of revealing what matters, later in the book. You may be surprised by how much of it you can actually omit.

- Do make sure that you revise it, though. Crime readers enjoy a mystery, and prefer to work things out themselves as they go along. Indulge them. Let your characters reveal themselves by what they say and do – don't divulge too much as you bring them on. In any case, your readers don't know these characters yet, so why would they care about their back stories? It's like somebody bombarding you with tales about a stranger you have never met: it's a cue to switch off, and you don't want your readers to do that.

Stephen King

'The most important things to remember about back story are that (a) everyone has a history and (b) most of it isn't very interesting.'

- The same principle applies to the fictional events that lead up to the crime. They are a kind of back story as well. When you've finished your first draft, you may well find that you've begun too soon and the plot really starts a good few pages in. In that case, you'll want to ditch your original opening and start in the right place – another reason for not spending too much time on it first time round.

- Most of all, it is much easier to write when there is already something on the page. Some writers spend months honing that single paragraph. Giving yourself permission to scrap the opening takes all the pressure off getting perfection on the page and lets you get on with the remainder of the book.

Write now

This is it, then. Write the first few pages of the novel that you have planned. If you've already done that – wonderful! Spend a half an hour writing the next bit. If you still haven't decided on a plot, use the body by the wall from the earlier chapters – perhaps in a different context, based on what you've learned so far, and use the next 'Write now' exercise to flesh out a proper plot. (If this turns out to be the novel you submit, you are welcome to the prompt.) But spend a half an hour right now getting something on the page.

Keep track of important elements as you develop the story

Once you have started writing in earnest, keep an eye on continuity. This matters. Here is what a commissioning editor has to say:

Linda Bennett, Crime editor, Salt Publishing

'Do be scrupulous about checking detail – that names of characters are consistent, and that sequences of events work, etc. All authors make slips, and it is an editor's job to spot these and point them out: but if I find too many mistakes during a first reading, I simply abandon the book.'

So:

- Keep a note of what you've said so far, or at least of where to find it. Until you are accomplished in the field, jot down a description of your characters so you don't give a suspect blue eyes in Chapter 1 and brown ones later on – unless that is a clue, and the character is not who they are pretending to be. Or note the page on which you describe the person first time round so that it is easy to refer to it again. Do the same for names and back stories. It may seem a nuisance when you're in the flow, but in the long run it saves a lot of time and it would be a pity to have your book rejected for such simple things.

- Keep a note of the presumptive dates you used in plots and subplots and a mental diary of events. Check against a calendar if you're in doubt. If it isn't crucial to the plot, you can make this part of your revision, if you choose. But do it sometime. That way you avoid somebody catching a commuter train on what turns out to be Sunday morning or a bank holiday, or performing an impossible sequence of actions in too short a time.

- Have a rough mental map of where things are and how long it would take to move between the different localities. Check that these are consistent in the narrative. If you can't visualize it strongly, draw the map. The back door mustn't open into the kitchen on page 4 and on to a passageway in Chapter 25.

- A reminder: keep track of your research. If you need to find out something before you can go on, stop and find it. If you can go round it, leave a space and go on writing while you are in the flow and then come back to it. When you find the answer, make a note of where – author, title and page number if you found it in a book, or the web address if you're on the Internet. That way you won't spend waste hours of your time trying to track it down again.

- Do the same for information that you find, think is interesting, and don't use straight away. If you think some snippet might be useful, make a note of where it was – don't just file it somewhere in your mind. This is a counsel of perfection, I'm aware, but it's born of painful experience.

Key idea

Keep a pad beside you for jotting down things to double-check, noting where in your manuscript to look for them. Keep a note of where you found the answers when you do.

- For your first novel, have a rough outline of your plot to hand showing at least the order of the main events. Once you have written a book or two, you can do this in your head. It will help you spread your plot points out across the book. Some people find it useful to make a careful plan – chapter by chapter – but if you're not that kind of planner, a general one will do.

- Make sure that you get all your important threads into the story fairly early on.

Write now

Provide yourself with a working outline of your own intended book using the five-step expansion technique outlined below. If you've already made a detailed plan, do this exercise in any case – it will help you when you come to writing a synopsis later on.

1 Start by writing a single sentence outlining the plot: 'X murders Y out of jealousy but Z (the sleuth) discovers this.'

2 Then break this down into smaller sentences, but adding relevant information as you go. First concentrate on 'X murders Y', adding details this time: the mode of death, the relationship between them and what kind of people they are (or were), and what drove X to do the crime right now.

3 Then write simple separate sentences about each of the other suspects that you have in mind, what relationship they had with the victim and the killer and what motives they might have.

4 Repeat the procedure, this time concentrating on the sleuth – who they are, what clues they discover, what false trails they follow and how they finally arrive at the truth – still making each item a sentence on its own.

5 Now shuffle the sentences so they represent the plot, aiming to space the information out across the book. If you're writing a thriller you can omit the shuffling, but mysteries require it if they are to work.

Keep this outline beside you as you work. It will prevent you putting too much of your plot at the beginning or at the end. Remember, though, that this is just a guide and not a straitjacket. If you get a better notion halfway through the book, tear up your remaining outline and write a different one.

Writer's block and how to deal with it

Writer's block is not a malady, or even an automatic side-effect of authorship. It's a state of mind. It often happens halfway through the book, when you lose impetus and interest in your characters or plot, or are simply stuck for where to go from here. Here are a few techniques for beating it. Many of them depend on thinking ahead.

Focus point

The best way to defeat writer's block is to prevent it happening, by taking steps to circumvent it when you're 'on a roll'.

- Leave a sentence uncompleted when you stop the day before. (I can't do this, but some people think it works.)
- Leave a scene uncompleted from one day to the next, though you know what happens next. As a variant on this, try deliberately stopping when you reach an exciting moment in the plot, even if you'd normally write for another half an hour. Next day you'll be eager to get back to it.
- Begin a session by revising what you wrote yesterday. (This one works for me.)
- Bring in a different character, new or otherwise, depending on where you are in the novel. This often gives you somewhere new to go and stops the feeling that you're stuck.
- If you have more than one viewpoint character, run the last scene from a different viewpoint in your head. Sometimes a different 'voice' will make the story flow more easily.
- Write an interruption into the story: a phone call, a visitor, a disturbance on the street. The interruption must be related to the plot, but it can serve to jerk-start the next bit of the book.
- If none of this works, read over what you've written so far. Are you content with it? Or is this block a message from your subconscious that you've taken a wrong turn? It may be as simple as a verb that isn't right, or a scene that's got rather static with not much happening. Locate the problem and you can deal with it. Sometimes just refreshing your memory like this will set you off again, with renewed enthusiasm for your original idea.
- Some people swear by jumping forward and writing a different scene that comes later in the book – then working back to where the block occurred. (If you're a methodical planner, this might be possible for you. I couldn't do it – I can't go on until I know what happened next.)
- Try writing something completely different, a letter to the tax office, a shopping list or duty 'thank you' notes – the more boring the better. This keeps you writing, which is what you want, and your story will seem more interesting when you get back to it.

- Go for a walk, have a drink and think of something else. But tomorrow come back and start from the first point again.
- If none of this is any help at all, there is only one solution. Tear up the last four pages that you wrote. Writer's block has been described as 'a name for what happens when you've bored yourself', and if the last bit's boring you, it's going to bore your readers, too. Don't tear up the whole of your manuscript in despair. Just scrap that last part and rewrite it, making it a bit more lively if you can. Or refer to your outline and shuffle it about – putting things in a slightly different order sometimes helps. If you're using a computer, open a new file and put the scrapped version in there – you never know when you might be able to use some of it again.

Writer's block is not incurable. It's just a state of mind. Don't lay claim to it among your friends because it's interesting, or use it as an excuse for not continuing to write.

Philip Pullman

'Writer's block… a lot of howling nonsense would be avoided if, in every sentence containing the word WRITER, that word was taken out and the word PLUMBER substituted; and the result examined for the sense it makes. Do plumbers get plumber's block? What would you think of a plumber who used that as an excuse not to do any work that day? The fact is that writing is hard work, and sometimes you don't want to do it, and you can't think of what to write next, and you're fed up with the whole damn business. Do you think plumbers don't feel like that about their work from time to time? Of course there will be days when the stuff is not flowing freely. What you do then is MAKE IT UP.'

The truth about revision and redrafting

There is going to be a lot of revision. It's part of the job of writing. All authors revise their work to some extent and quite often it's the most successful ones who do it most. You may be revising as you go along, but once you have completed your first draft, read the whole thing through and then begin the second part of the writing task – revising what you've done.

Here are some of the things to look for as you work:

- Redraft that opening for maximum effect.
- Double-check the items on your jotter list.
- Check continuity.
- Aim to cut your longest sentences in half.
- Look for the longest paragraphs and reduce them if you can.
- Go on an adverb-and-adjective hunt – see how many you can capture and remove.
- Challenge yourself to get rid of extra verbiage, unnecessary descriptions and dialogue that isn't working for its keep.
- Cut out or conceal excess research that shows.

- Work for changes of pace and style.
- Read it aloud to yourself. Check for jerky rhythm, accidentally repeated words, and passages that you find difficult to say – they are also difficult to read. Try different voices for the dialogue and see whether it rings true. Your housemates and neighbours may suppose you're mad, but it's a good way of making yourself read with care.
- Check that you've applied the techniques outlined in this book.
- Ask yourself the question every page or two: do I believe this? Is it credible? If not, go back and work that scene again.
- 'Murder your darlings.'
- Lastly, make sure that you check your alterations against the whole. It's easy to change something during a revision and forget that this has repercussions for other passages.

Focus point

Revising a manuscript is like pruning a rose bush. Cut back superfluous growth, eliminate things that interfere with good development, encourage your strongest side shoots, and trim the whole thing to get a better shape.

Workshop exercise

Here's a short questionnaire to help you see what to revise, if anything.

1   How soon in the story does the death occur (or the threat, if it's a thriller)? Can I make it any sooner? Would that be a good idea?

2   How many red herrings or false dawns occur? Red herrings are false trails, of course. False dawns occur in thrillers when rescue or lifting of the threat seems imminent, only to be thwarted by the villain or events. In a crime novel a false dawn is when the sleuth or someone else appears to have a solution for the crime that later proves untenable. (This is not the same as a red herring. It may be the right answer for the wrong reasons, the wrong answer for the right reasons or only a partial answer.) Do I need more red herrings or false dawns? Or fewer? Are mine credible?

3   How many suspects are there (if I'm writing mystery)? Do they all have a strong enough motive, and some opportunity?

4   How pressing is the threat (if I'm writing a thriller)? Is there a sufficient sense of urgency and have I built the tension by showing the inevitable progress towards some dire event?

5   Where in the text have I concealed my clues or the weaknesses in the plan my villain has devised? Do those paragraphs read like normal prose, or is it evident that they are pivotal?

6   Is the middle sagging? What can I do to give it impetus?

7   How close to the end does the denouement occur? If it's a mystery, have I spread out the exposition well enough – is

there enough action in the final part? If I'm working on a thriller, does the 'escape' ring true, and is it the result of action, not an accident? Is there too much action at the very end or do I need a cool-down paragraph or two?

Apply these questions to your manuscript. But not until you've finished the first draft.

When you have revised your story once, read it through again. If there is any scene that you're still struggling with, have one more go at redrafting it, but keep both versions and compare them afterwards. Sometimes you will find that first thoughts were best, because they were freshest. Select the better version and let it go at that. Then move on to look for technical mistakes.

Doing a technical edit

This is different from revision. You are not changing anything, you are just correcting it. It may seem boring but don't ignore this step. It makes a big difference to how your manuscript is received. And don't suppose that you won't need it. Everybody makes small mistakes – of course they do. And it's your job to correct them, not an agent's or an editor's. Their job is only to pick up the ones you didn't spot – and there will almost certainly still be a few of those. If you want them to read the manuscript at all, pay them the compliment of correcting what you can. If you can't be bothered to spend time and care on what you write, why should an agent or a publisher?

Focus point

A final technical edit is the last part of the writing task.

Edit exercise

Look at the novel opening that you wrote at the beginning of this chapter. Underline any misspellings or typos you can spot, and decide whether the punctuation is correct. Look especially at any dialogue. Then make the corrections. How many were there, if any?

So, to do a technical edit, what are we looking for?

CHECK FOR SPELLING ERRORS

Use a good dictionary if you are in any doubt. Don't rely solely on the spell-check function on your computer. Although it may help with typos, which can otherwise be hard to spot because you tend to see what you expect to see, it will let any word slide through if it exists, regardless of the sense, or – worse – change your misspelt word to something else you didn't mean at all.

Snapshot exercise

Here are a list of five words that are frequently misspelt and three sentences containing words or expressions that are commonly confused. Make sure that you know which is the correct spelling and meaning in each case.

- Occasionally or occaisionally?
- Apparantly or apparently?
- Sentence or sentance?
- Musn't or mustn't?
- Thourough or thorough?
- Are you inferring by your question that I'm wrong? (Or should that be 'implying'?)
- The temperature of the room affects the speed of rigor mortis. (Or should that be 'effects'?)
- The time of the accident begs the question of what he was doing there. (Or should that be 'raises the question'?)

Are there any spellings and expressions that you get wrong? Even lecturers in English grammar have a few! Make a reminder list of your personal top ten and keep it beside you to refer to. You'll be glad you did.

CHECK PUNCTUATION, TOO

If you are not sure how to punctuate, you will find some useful handbooks listed in the Appendix. You can either acquire a copy of your own or ask at your library.

DO IT YOURSELF

Some novice authors like to get a friend to check for these mistakes, but my advice is – don't. Friends either flatter or play devil's advocate. Neither is very helpful at this point – you are looking for technical assistance not critical reviews. If you've a friend who is a writer too, you might exchange your services on the understanding that neither (at this stage) wants comments on the text. There are also people who will do it professionally, for a fee. But checking spelling and punctuation is useful to learn – you are going to need it later when you get the page proofs, so treat this as an opportunity to acquire the skill.

Snapshot exercise

Hone your skills by practising on the paragraph below. Don't cheat and linger over it, just read it through quickly – exactly as you would read through your own manuscript – and see how many errors (if any) you can find. Please don't write them down; just keep a mental count. And read it once only – you'll see why later on.

When your looking through your manuscript for technical mistakes you might find it help to start at the bottom of the page – or the end of a chapter on a computer screen – and read upwards. Its earier to see errors when you aren't distracted by the sense. Highlight the errors as you go or note the line numbers on your jotter pad so you know were they are if you don't want to stop and correct them there and then. Don't make your technical edit til you've done any redrafting you want, or you'll have to do it again when the manuscript in it's final form.

Snapshot exercise

Repeat the Snapshot exercise above again, but this time use the technique that the paragraph describes, starting at the bottom and reading backwards through the text. Do it now, before you read the rest of this.

How many errors did you find this time? Did reading backwards help? You'll find the errors listed in the Appendix. If you missed any this time, make a note of what they were – that's likely to be the kind you're most prone to overlook.

When to stop tinkering with your manuscript and send it in

Now. That's right. When you have finished your technical edit – stop. You can go on fiddling with it for months without improving things. And it won't magically transmute by lying in a drawer. It's time to bite the bullet and start submitting it.

Where to next?

You've made your work the best that you can make it, for now at any rate. There's no point in tinkering any more. If anyone wants your novel, they will probably ask you to revise it again, in any case. Be delighted, not affronted, if that turns out to be the case. It's a sign that someone has seen promise in your work. But first you have to send it in and win their interest. That is the subject of Chapter 10.

10

Preparing for publication

When you have written and revised your novel, don't put it in a drawer. You haven't really finished till you've submitted it.

John Campbell

'The reason 99% of all stories written are not bought by editors is very simple. Editors never buy manuscripts that are left on the closet shelf at home.'

Why you should finish your novel before you submit anything

You may have heard – correctly – that many agents and publishers ask you to submit a synopsis and the first three chapters rather than the whole novel. That doesn't mean that you should write just those, and not bother to finish it until you get some interest. Finish the novel first, before you send it – or any part of it – to anyone. Here are some reasons why:

- If you do get someone interested, they are going to want the rest. Immediately. Not in ten months' time, when you have finished it. Ask them to wait while you get it written, and you make it clear that you haven't yet got anything to sell. The chances are that they'll lose interest straight away.

- An agent may just possibly take a chance on you and invite you to submit the book again when you have finished – but an expression of interest is not a contract. With crime, which depends so much on sustaining a good plot, publishers generally want to see the whole thing before they will commit to a first-time novelist.

Dorothy Lumley, late founder of the Dorian Literary Agency

'I can get an idea of how good a writer is from looking at the first few pages of a manuscript, but I only know how good a crime writer they are when I have had a chance to see them working through the plot.'

- Those three chapters that you're going to send will be much better when they've been revised. That means after you've done the rest, improved your skills and know exactly what the opening should contain.

- You don't want to tie yourself to a synopsis if you haven't finished the book. As you write and the characters and plot develop, you may get better ideas than the ones you started with. You can then offer that version when you submit. When you've sold a few crime stories, it won't matter if you don't entirely stick to your synopsis – but the first time, that's what you're reckoning to sell. You'll be expected to deliver it.

- Tell yourself you'll only have to do it this way once. It's commitment, sure – but once you've sold one book successfully, the chances are that next time you can sell them an idea.

Do you need an agent?

Yes, you do – if you hope to be published by a mainstream publisher. This is for several reasons:

- Lots of publishing houses won't even look at a novel that has not been sent to them by an agent. This is what they mean when they say 'no unsolicited manuscripts'. This is not because they're being difficult. A publishing house has limited resources. Their business is publishing books and they can't afford to pay their editors to spend time sifting through the wholly unsuitable. If they accept only agented work, the first level of filter has been for done for them.

- Even the few mainstream publishing houses that will accept unsolicited manuscripts (for example, the UK publisher Robert Hale is good to newcomers) will not rush yours upstairs to a commissioning editor. They'll put it with a hundred others on the 'slush pile'. It will be read, when it rises to the top, by an underpaid and overworked junior who has hundreds more to look at and lots of other urgent jobs to do, like making tea and sorting through the post. Even if that junior likes it, they don't have authority to rush it into print, only pass it up to the next layer in the hierarchy for consideration there. A submission by an agent bypasses all that.

- Part of an agent's job is to know which publishing house is likely to be most receptive to your kind of book. You can find out a certain amount yourself from the *Writers' & Artists' Yearbook*, for instance, or by studying everything they print, but that is a long process and editors may change. An agent will know the people involved, their personal tastes and personalities, so is much more likely to achieve a good match.

- An agent will also know what you cannot know yourself – that is what similar works are in the pipeline from any publisher. No one will warn you before they've read what you submit that they've already commissioned a crime series set in the Hebrides, so they are unlikely to be interested in your attempt. An agent, through contacts, will very soon find out and not waste time sending your manuscript to them.

Key idea

An agent has a vested interest in assisting you.

- Agents make money by selling manuscripts. There's no commission until they've sold your work. So if they take you on they'll help you. They'll tell you where to revise and edit to make sure that your work is good enough, advise you when and where to cut, and then go off and argue your cause with publishers. All this for 10 or 15 per cent of what you earn.
- Plus, with any luck, they'll sell you into other markets, too. An agent will handle your overseas and translation rights – British and US crime novels are popular worldwide. They usually handle serialization, film, large print and e-book rights, if those are not already covered by your contract with the publisher.
- An agent takes on an author, unlike a publisher who only takes the book. Find a good agent and you will have a champion, a critic, a vocational counsellor and, in the long run, probably a friend. When my agent – with whom I had worked for 20 years – died very recently, I was bereft. Even after more than 20 novels, I was anxious and anchorless until I found another one.

A few specialist crime publishers (like SALT in the UK) say that you can send your manuscript direct, and that there is no significant bias in favour of those submitted by an agent. They also often tell you to send in the entire manuscript, not just three chapters and a synopsis. As publishers, they won't commission until they've seen the whole thing. This is still not an argument for going it alone in my view, for all the reasons that are listed above.

Focus point

Many publishers refuse to accept submissions that aren't agented – but no publishing house I've heard of refuses to consider manuscripts that are. So get yourself an agent if you can.

How to approach an agent

- Look in the *Writers' & Artists' Yearbook* or the *Macmillan Palgrave Writers' Handbook* or the *Writer's Market* for agents who specialize in crime – in particular the kind of crime you've tried to write. Or use the Internet – but double-check to make sure that the agency is legitimate.

- Most agencies list their most famous clients, so let that be a guide. Choose one that doesn't represent the big names in the field unless you are very talented or very brave. Such agents are inundated by the hopeful, but a book would have to be exceptional for them to take it on. They'll read your manuscript, eventually, of course – nobody wants to find that they've turned the new 'big thing' – and if they do take you, they'll look after you, but nurturing modest talent is not what they're about. Put yourself in the agent's shoes. You get 10 to 15 per cent of what your client earns. Are you going to devote yourself more to fostering a multi-million bestseller or a first-time unknown?

- Find someone with a modest stable, someone starting out, a new appointment in an agency – or, best of all, someone just branching out and setting up on their own. If they've already worked in a bigger agency, they'll know the business and won't be learning as they go. New agents need new writers, so these are the people actively looking for new clients. If you can get in at the beginning, you have the maximum chance.

- An individual agent is often a good choice. They have to make a living rather than enjoying a salary irrespective of how many books they don't accept and that means selling manuscripts to publishers.

- If you opt for a bigger company, write to a named person, not just the agency. You can check who works there on the Internet, or by looking in the handbooks, as above. If you can't find the information you need from there, it is acceptable to ring and ask which agent handles crime.

- Don't try to find an agent on the telephone. It is permissible to ring up an agency to confirm that they are reading new submissions at the moment (if they say their list is full, it's probably the case) and, if so, to ask how much of the manuscript they would like to see.

- It is nowadays more or less acceptable (though not obligatory) to send a submission to several agencies at once. If you do that, observe the expected etiquette. If you get interest from anyone, let the others know at once. It gives them a chance to compete for you, if they've decided to accept your book.

- You don't want to make dozens of copies of your submission, so be discriminate. The best technique is probably the 'cascade technique'. Make a list of possibilities, starting with the agent you'd most like to be with and adding the others in descending order. Then apply to the first three on your list, at intervals of about a week or so apart. If you get a rejection from any one of them, send your submission straight off again – this time to your fourth choice and so on down the list. Keep a record of which ones have replied, and if you haven't heard from a particular agency within six weeks or so, print out your material again and send it to someone else.

- Once you've sent your submission off, keep an open mind. It may be that the delay is because you're still being considered. Thousands of people write to agents every year. Reading all those manuscripts can take a little while, so don't expect an answer by return of post. Ringing or otherwise pestering the agency is a good way of getting your manuscript returned. Only contact them if months have passed, in case it has got lost. A way to find out whether it has been received is to send an SAE and ask them to return that as an acknowledgement of receipt.

- Don't write to agents who make it clear that they don't handle the sort of crime you write, just because they're close to where you live or because you've heard of them. You would be surprised how many people do. Some would-be authors start at the beginning of the handbook list and simply bombard everyone in turn. It isn't courteous – agents still have to reply instead of dealing with their proper clientele – and it is a waste of everybody's time.

- Give yourself an edge over the opposition by making your query letter and submission package as professional as you can. When approaching an agent at this stage you should send:

  - the first three chapters of your manuscript

  - a synopsis – no longer than a page or two at most

  - a covering letter

  - a stamped self-addressed envelope for a reply, and enough postage for the return of your material.

And that's all. No photographs, copies of nice remarks your friends have made, no general CV. You will sometimes encounter the advice to include a memory stick or disk containing the whole novel, but that's a recipe for having it get lost. Some agents think it looks presumptuous, as though you're expecting them to spend time downloading it. If they don't like your printed chapters, they won't read it anyway. Just offer to send one if they want to see the rest and would prefer to have it in that form.

Dorothy Lumley, late founder of the Dorian Literary Agency

'I want to see enough of the work of a prospective author to make sure that they can write and enough of a synopsis to make sure that there's a plot. If I'm impressed with that, I will ask to see the rest. I also want it decently presented so it's convenient to read. I don't really want it on a disk and I certainly don't want it emailed in some format which I can't download. And I don't want to be hectored if I keep it for a week.'

Snapshot exercise

Do it now. Use whatever means you have available and find the names and contact addresses of at least six agents who say they handle crime.

I could, of course, have put them in the appendix to this book but, by the time you're reading this, that information may no longer be accurate. There's already one less agent that I know about.

Submitting the first three chapters

So what will this submission consist of? You may read that an agency requires 'three sample chapters'. They mean the first three, for a fiction book. With non-fiction it is sometimes different, because they want to see the breadth of your approach. But with novels, and particularly crime, the agent wants to get a feel of how the story flows. In reality, this means seeing what the opening is like, and whether you can keep that pace and tension and afterwards. So:

- Send the first three chapters and only those, even if you think a later one is more indicative of how well you can write. Think of it as making clear that you can follow simple instructions.
- Make sure that you turn in a decently presented manuscript. It must be typed, double-spaced and with sizeable margins all around the text – agents sometimes make notes in the margins of points they want to raise. If you write on a computer – and most people do – don't choose a fancy font (Times is usual, though I use Helvetica). Number the pages, adding what is called a 'strap' on every sheet, giving your name (or writing name) and the proposed title of the book. Edit the manuscript carefully before you print it out.
- Print it on one side only of standard A4 paper. Put the sheets in order, but keep them separate. Don't put them in a ringbinder or staple them together down one side. You can put them loose in a plastic folder if you like, or use an elastic band or paperclip. The same goes for the whole manuscript when you submit it later on.
- Add a title page (see below).

Snapshot exercise

Finding a title is not as easy as it might appear and is probably best done when your manuscript is in its final form. Even if you've already got a title in your head, please do this exercise. You may think of something snappier, and it may come in useful later – see below.

Take five minutes to brainstorm all the words and phrases you can think of in connection with your setting, plot and characters. Include such words as 'murder', 'death' or 'kidnapping' – whatever fits the bill. When you have made your list, combine the items in lots of different ways until you hit on something which strikes a chord with you. Make that your working title, but keep the list you made. Be warned that your editor or agent may not like your first choice much because it's been done, is too short, too long, doesn't fit in with house style, or doesn't excite the marketing department. This exercise will help you if you have to think again.

Preparing a title page

- Print the proposed title in the centre of the page.
- Underneath it, on a separate line, indicate the approximate word count of the whole book. Don't rely on the computer word count here. What the publisher will eventually want to know is how many pages they are going to have to allow for and that is a different calculation. Also, this assures the agent that you have a completed manuscript to sell. (For how to do a word count, see the Snapshot exercise that follows this section.)
- Below that write 'sample chapters' and, on the line below, your name.
- Then put your address that on the right-hand bottom corner of the sheet.
- Finally, you can add the letter 'c' discreetly on the bottom line (or the copyright sign if you have that on your keyboard) followed by your initial, surname and the year. Don't write 'copyright' in full, or emblazon your work with 'all rights reserved' or similar. Any of that will mark you as a novice straight away. Your work is copyright in any case, though there is no copyright (ever) on titles or ideas. But don't let that deter you. Your prospective agent doesn't want to steal your plot – they want to sell your novel and make money out of you.
- Position this sheet so that it forms the first page of the manuscript, and turn your attention to the synopsis.

Snapshot exercise

Do a practice word count. Take four random complete pages from your manuscript. Manually count the total number of words on those four pages and then divide by four, to work out the average number of words per page. Then multiply that by the number of pages in your manuscript, round it to the nearest thousand, and that's the 'approximate word count' that you're looking for.

If you are not working on a computer, where the number of lines per page is fairly standard, you'll have an extra job. You'll first have to work out the average number of words per line, and then the average lines per page before you can proceed as above.

Don't worry that some pages may be very short of print – they will be in the published version, too. Make a note of the total, and see whether you need to cut or edit, as below.

Edit exercise

If the total word count comes to much more than 80,000, your novel is probably too long. Look at it and see what you can profitably cut. If it comes to much less than 60,000, you may need to add another scene. Finding another 'false dawn' may be a way of doing this. Make any alterations that your manuscript requires.

Writing a synopsis

Key idea

A synopsis is not a quickly written outline of the plot. It is the bait to catch an agent and – you hope – a publisher.

I have seen advice to would-be novelists arguing that you needn't send a synopsis with your sample chapters nowadays. This may seem tempting, but does not apply to you. Crime, as usual, is a special case. No one is going to make an offer for your work without being certain that you can sustain a plot, so, if you're not sending the whole manuscript, you will need a synopsis.

There are a few points to keep in mind:

- Make it fairly brief. More than a page or two is probably too much, half a page is better if you can squeeze in enough information.
- Start by deciding what is different and special about your narrative. Is it the setting? An inside knowledge of forensic medicine? Action? Suspense? Or hard-hitting detail? Get that idea in the short first paragraph, along with a description of the crime.
- Also give the name of the victim of the crime and a very brief statement of who that person was in life and what kind of role and personality they had. Or, if this is a thriller, why they are vulnerable or at risk. Highlight the names of major characters, by using capitals or underlining them.
- Devote a similar sentence to your sleuth, or rescuer, if you have one. Sketch in any conflict that these characters might have with colleagues, and include a one-word statement of any flaws they have. The intention is to show that these are rounded characters.
- Now add a short statement about each suspect, if this is a whodunnit, and suggest what kind of motive each might have.

If it's a whydunnit, explain the triggers that give rise to the crime. If it is a thriller, describe how the threat develops, or how the initial kidnapping is carried out. If you have more than one viewpoint, you can say so here. In all subgenres, stress psychological dimensions. You want to make these people seem as lively as you can.

- Mention any red herrings and false dawns. These are the proof that there are twists and turns and that the plot won't sag in the middle of the book.

- Account for how your protagonist prevails. Bold action? Interviews? Quick thinking? Seeing clues? Confrontation with the criminal? Don't, however, spell these out in detail. The idea is to give a flavour of the book but leave something for the reader to find out.

- End with the statement that the crime is solved or the threat averted, making it clear that you understand the 'rules'. What you do not have to do is to announce the answer, and say who actually 'dunnit', and exactly how, or even why. The same principle applies to thrillers, too – you needn't give full details of how the threat is averted. Of course, you may do so if you wish, but I prefer to leave something as a lure. You want to make your target – whether agent or publisher – keen to read the rest.

- Type it up nicely, check it for mistakes, and add it to your package, but don't put it with the manuscript. Attach it to the letter, which we'll look at after this …

Workshop exercise

Read through this synopsis, then answer the questionnaire that follows it.

JOHN MARSHALL, a Cheltenham businessman, is a self-made millionaire so when he is discovered strangled in a dingy empty flat, the police put their most experienced inspector on the case. D.I. BILL RANSOM is new to the locality, having had a successful but turbulent career in Birmingham, where his maverick tendencies have seen him get spectacular results. Anxious to make a fresh start in a difference place, Ransom begins by playing by the book, meekly interviewing friends and relatives, and patiently submitting to tedious reports from the scene of crime officer (the attractive but acerbic JENNIFER FORD) and the pathologist – which tell him nothing new.

Marshall was a ruthless man, with many enemies. But who hated him enough to strangle him? Ex-business partner PETER WYATT, manoeuvred into selling out to Marshall at considerable loss, just when the business was about to boom? Marshall's nephew MARTIN ALLSOP, who recently lost both fiancée and home after his uncle ruthlessly called in a loan? Or RALPH HITCHENS, the ineffectual schoolteacher whose adored wife SANDRA Marshall lured away into a trophy marriage, which she admits herself was a mistake? Marshall, she says, had been unfaithful from the very start, and had boasted of a string of mistresses, though he was tiring of his current conquest – the beautiful and wilful ANGELINA GREEN, whom he had been keeping in some style in the town.

Ransom's enquiries reveal that Marshall was last seen leaving his offices shortly after five the day he died. Forensics say that he was dead by ten. Sandra declares he did not come home that night – though that was no surprise, as he often didn't. In fact she'd given up at eight, and gone to talk to Ralph, at his request – and there were doubtless people who had seen them in the pub. Angelina had been expecting him, but didn't see him either and went out in disgust, using the theatre tickets he had bought for her. Neither Peter nor Martin have any alibi.

Two of Sandra's neighbours claim there was a row next door, and they saw Marshall driving from his own house that evening – though they give conflicting evidence about the time that this occurred. When Ransom realizes that both of them are right, and that a key found in the corpse's pocket is an important clue, he is able to unmask the murderer.

1 How many words does this synopsis use?

2 In what ways is it not an outline of the plot?

3 How many characters does it specify?

4 How many other characters are implied?

5 How much do you know about the corpse?

6 How much do you know about the sleuth?

7 How much do you know about the suspects in the case?

8 How many different settings are mentioned, or suggested, in the text?

9 What is the function of writing some names in capitals?

10 What is the function of writing JENNIFER FORD in capitals?

11 Are there any subplots implied or actual?

12 Any idea who did it?

Write now

Now it's your turn. Write a synopsis of your own novel ready to submit. Try to keep it under 2,000 words. You can use your computer this time to count the words for you.

The covering letter – what to put in and what to leave out of it

Your covering letter should be:

- **Short** – the agent wants to read the book, not another treatise about you.
- **Polite** – short does not mean peremptory. You are asking the agent to spend their working time on you, rather than another candidate. There's no harm in saying that you 'would be very grateful' if they would consider the enclosed. Express a willingness to submit your work in any other form convenient, if they wish to see the rest.
- **Professional,** which means leaving out things that are not relevant. Don't mention your education or employment history unless it's either quite exceptional or in some way related to the book. For example, if you are a forensic scientist, it is of course relevant. Being a schoolteacher or a member of a reading group is not. Don't say how much your friends and relatives have liked the book, or how you have always wanted to be a writer.

Remember to include the following:

- Do mention why you chose this agency – because it represents someone whose work you admire, because you've heard of it, or you understand that they are seeking new authors at this time. This indicates that you have done some relevant research.

- Do mention any publication history, even if in completely different fields. If you're a member of the Writers' Guild, the Society of Authors, Romantic Novelists, or any other professional writers' body, say so. Similarly, mention if you've ever won a prize for something that you wrote since you left school.
- Writing courses you've attended might be relevant and show that you are serious about the craft, but don't list too many or you will look like a wannabe. Don't bother mentioning writers' circles here – they mostly exist for mutual support, though it's not a bad idea to belong to one.
- Do write a closing sentence saying what's enclosed, for example, 'the first three chapters and synopsis for a [specify the genre here – thriller, noir whodunnit, police procedural or whatever applies] with the working title "X".' This shows that you have some understanding of the field and – by saying 'working title' – that you're prepared to take advice.
- Point out that you've enclosed return postage for the manuscript and an SAE for acknowledgement of receipt, then finish by saying that you hope to hear from them – and leave it at that.
- Sign off with 'Yours sincerely' if you've approached someone by name; otherwise use 'Yours faithfully'. Next time, if there is a next time, you can send your 'kind regards'.
- That's all. Make sure that it's properly set out and not full of typos and grammatical mistakes. This letter is the first piece of your writing that the agent will see – make sure that it is a good advertisement.

Snapshot exercise

Take five minutes to write down a short list of any special experiences you've had, including things like local knowledge or nursing training which might be relevant to writing crime and which you could mention in a covering letter to an agency. Add any publishing history you've had, even if it was only in the local magazine, and any writing courses you've been on. Keep the list on file, and add to it if anything else comes to mind. If you think your list is looking particularly thin, do things that will add to it. Attend a weekend writing course, perhaps, or contribute something to your local magazine. Give yourself a writing history. Every little helps.

Write now

Write a covering letter for your manuscript. Make this a practice if you're not ready to submit yet. If you work on a computer, store it as a file and use it when you're ready, or use it as a template for your next attempt, if your first submission fails. Make sure that you take time to edit for mistakes, remembering the techniques that we looked at earlier.

Now put the whole submission into a sturdy envelope and add your SAE for acknowledgement of receipt and an address label with sufficient postage for return. If you've used the right kind of envelope, they'll probably use that to send it back. Then post it, go back to your computer or typewriter, and start working on the next book that you're going to write.

Being realistic – what are my chances of success?

It's always possible that you will be taken up at once and become an overnight success. It happens. Someone has to be the 'next big thing' and, if you are both talented and extremely fortunate, it might just be you. You might also win the lottery or be struck by lightning. However, it's much more likely that life won't turn out like that.

In some ways it's more difficult to sell a manuscript than it has ever been. Finding an agent is difficult enough and persuading a publisher to invest in you is harder still. However, if your book has promise, you are likely to find someone in the end to take you on. The key words here are 'in the end'. Don't be disappointed if you get rejections first. Almost every bestseller, from *Watership Down* to the first Harry Potter book, was turned down initially, and not just once but sometimes scores of times. The trick is to keep on trying and start working on something else.

Barbara Kingsolver, novelist

'This manuscript of yours that has just come back from another editor is a precious package. Don't consider it rejected. Consider that you've addressed it "to the editor who can appreciate my work" and it has simply come back stamped "Not at this address". Just keep looking for the right address.'

If you get a nice letter from an agency – or publisher if you have sent it to one who buys direct – saying that your work has promise but is not for them, take that as a serious compliment. The standard rejection is just a printed form. If you also get suggestions about what's wrong with it and how you could make it better, that is even more encouraging. Agents (or editors) don't waste time offering advice to authors who have no future. So, if that happens, go away and do as they suggest, before you send it to anybody else. Some people even advocate sending it back to whoever made the comment, showing that you have taken their advice.

Even when you've found an agent there is no guarantee that the novel will be published, though it multiplies the chances to a huge degree.

Bookshops are closing by the dozen every year and those that remain are usually big chains that have agreements with major publishers to put certain titles in the window or in some other prominent display. The publisher actually pays for this in order to advertise their wares. This makes it really hard for agents to push their newcomers. Besides, there are now fewer mainstream publishers and many different imprints are owned by the same few giant parent companies.

But things are not as bad as this suggests. Bookselling is not dead. More money was spent on books in the UK in 2013 than on buying bread. Hundreds of titles are still published every month and publishers know their business. There's still a market out there – though more of it is in the supermarkets and on Amazon these days.

And here is the really interesting bit. Crime fiction is extremely popular worldwide. New fans are being added every day. Editors are always looking for the fresh new voice and something different. So you have a better chance than newcomers in other genres, and maybe better even than some mid-list crime authors. Publishers are ruthless about dropping authors who no longer fit their list, or haven't enjoyed the popular success that they were looking for. So grit your teeth and prepare to battle through.

Focus point

New crime writers have a better chance of getting published than most other newcomers.

How to deal with rejection

John Scalzi

'Engrave this in your brain: EVERY WRITER GETS REJECTED. You will be no different.'

Don't let rejection put you off too much. Remind yourself that we all have different tastes. Did you like every book you ever read? So when your submission package comes back to you, give a deep sigh, make sure that the contents are looking clean and fresh (coffee stains and doodles are a giveaway that someone else has just rejected it), write a new covering letter and send it off again. Then go back writing that next one. And that's not just to take your mind off things. Agents like to know that an author has a new work in progress – it gives promise that you're not a 'one-book wonder'.

Other possibilities for getting published

If you can't find an agent, there are other ways to get published. The decline in the number of mainstream publishers, and the fact that supermarkets sell as many books as some booksellers, has meant that a lot more people are going it alone. There are a growing number of small independent presses and genre specialists, and burgeoning online opportunities as well.

SMALL PRESSES

A lot of these are run by individuals trying to publish a few titles that they believe in, rather than being guided by what they think will sell. Most of them don't deal with crime, though there are one or two that do – and with considerable success. These imprints aren't usually stocked by major bookshop chains, at least not nationally, but online sales are growing all the time.

But do be courteous. If you decide to submit your novel to one of the small presses, be especially careful to research what kind of submissions they are looking for. Don't send to companies that don't handle crime. A small company like this has even less time than other publishers to waste on people who haven't the courtesy to find out what they want.

DIGITAL SELF-PUBLISHING

There are a number of companies that advertise online and that will always publish your book for you – for a fee. This used to be called 'vanity publishing' and was something to be avoided because it was expensive and no attempt was ever made to market anything, so you ended up with a garage full of books which nobody would buy. These days things are rather different. There is no longer the huge outlay that there used to be, partly because electronic printing methods make this viable. Most of these companies will produce a book for you which looks halfway decent (although you can usually spot a vanity publisher by the quality of the typesetting and print) and even get it on to Amazon (and sometimes into your nearest bookshop) usually with an e-book version, too.

It is still vanity publishing, and you still pay for it – but it's one way of ensuring that you do get into print.

SELF-PUBLISHING

You can, of course, cut out the middleman and become a publisher yourself. This involves a huge amount of work, as you are responsible for everything from editing and design to marketing it afterwards. You can do this the old-fashioned way, by ordering multiple copies of your book from a printer, or approach a print-on-demand company like Lulu, which makes the process much more affordable. Or you can simply publish your novel as an e-book, through Amazon or Smashwords or something similar. Be warned, though, that there are laws regarding publishing. Even if you are only publishing online, you will have to apply and pay for an IBSN number (in fact, you can only buy them in blocks of ten) and you will also be liable for tax – though, of course, you will not have publishers and agents deducting their percentages.

Some people have had huge successes doing this, especially in the early days of e-publishing, though admittedly in other genres than crime. However, you might always be the first. If you know a lot about marketing and production, and really love a challenge, then this may be for you. Remember, though, that publishing a book, getting it reviewed and marketed out into the shops, to say nothing of keeping meticulous accounts of all your costs, is much more difficult – and far more time-consuming – than writing it.

NON-COMMERCIAL 'PUBLISHING'

If you only want to write for fun, and don't care whether you sell your book or not, there are websites where you can share your work with other amateurs. There is no problem of rejection there, of course, and other people's comments can be quite valuable. But if you really want to call yourself a crime writer, get your book into print.

What happens next?

What happens when you have found an agent and they have sold your book? You will sign a contract with the publishers, agreeing to submit 'a manuscript of publishable quality' by a given date – which should be all right because you've already written it. In return, they promise to print a certain quantity, to distribute the copies and to pay you for your work. Don't expect a six-figure offer here. Generally there is modest 'advance' up front, followed by a percentage royalty, payable only after you have earned back the advance.

Don't worry if the sum appears unreasonably small. The bigger the advance, the more copies you have to sell before royalties begin. The only advantage of a larger advance is that, if the title doesn't sell, you generally don't have to pay it back. An exception might be when publishers spend more money on publicizing the authors to whom they've given the most generous advance because they want to earn their investment money back.

Your advance may well be broken into even smaller sums, part payable on signature, some on completion and some on publication. That depends on the company, and it is your agent's job to see that you get the best terms available. The contract may involve the sale of other rights – film, large print and so on – and a promise that, if the title is remaindered, you will have the opportunity to buy copies back at the remaindered price.

You will then be working with an editor who will very likely want you to revise your book again. You can argue, if you must, but only on really important issues. (My first editor wanted me to cut a line – not in a crime novel – which seemed critical to me. It is still there and the book has since been reprinted many times.) Find another title if they want you to, and if they suggest you cut your favourite scene, they probably know best. They are not out to spoil your efforts, but to make them sell. When they are happy with the whole effect, they'll want a totally clean version of the text – these days this tends to be on disk or sent as file attachment to an email. They check it over and send it off to print.

A little later you will get the galley proofs. This is a copy of the typeset version of your work, which will require the kind of technical edit that we looked at earlier. This is called a copy-edit, and other people will be doing it as well. Be particularly careful where you've changed the text as part of the revision as that's where errors frequently occur. There are conventions for marking up the corrections, you'll find them in the *Writers' & Artists' Yearbook* for easy reference.

When the book is published, you'll get a specified number of free copies (usually six, but occasionally more), one of which will have to go to your agent straight away. After that you have to buy your copies from the publisher, though at a discounted price. Friends and family often don't appreciate this fact, and expect you to give them all a signed copy of your book.

Your first book may well warrant a review, perhaps even in the newspapers, but unless you're very successful that won't happen every time. And then it goes on sale. You may be asked to sign some copies for a bookshop, or to give a talk at a local festival. Do so if you can. It draws attention to your work and brings you readers. After all, you are now a crime writer.

For a more complete guide to getting published, you can try *Masterclass: Get Your Book Published* by Katherine Lapworth, which is in the same series as this title.

Snapshot exercise

As a final exercise, revisit the Snapshot exercise you did in the Introduction to this book, in which you were asked to write down the three important things you hoped to learn from it. Look back at your answers now and write down the three things that you *have* got from it.

Appendix: bibliography

If you have been interested in the content of this book, here are a few suggestions for further reading, divided into sections for ease of reference. Most of these books are still in print – and/or on Kindle – and available through Amazon or the Book Depository. The dates given are for the latest edition, where possible.

This list is not exhaustive: you could add to it yourself if you go online, but these are books that have either been invaluable to me, or were useful to one or more of my writing students. You will probably not want to read them all (that becomes a displacement activity for writing) but you will find additional sources here for topics in the text (including specialist crime topics) and books that will give you additional guidance on punctuation, presentation and style. Some titles on the list you will probably want to own and will return to, time after time, if you keep on writing books. Where I think that's the case, I've mentioned it.

General writing guidelines

Aitken, Rosemary, *Writing a Novel: A Practical Guide* (Crowood Press, 2003) – this is me, wearing my general author's hat.

Armstrong, David, *How Not to Write a Novel* (Allison and Busby, 2003) – amusing and still apt.

Block, Lawrence, *Telling Lies for Fun and Profit* (William Morrow Paperbacks, 1994) – entertaining, but some tips regarding submissions etc., apply only in the United States.

Braine, John, *How to Write a Novel* (Methuen, 1974) – an older book with continuing appeal.

Frey, James N., *How to Write a Damn Good Novel: A Step-by-step No-nonsense Guide to Dramatic Story-telling* (St. Martin's Press, 1989)

King, Stephen, *On Writing: A Memoir of the Craft* (Hodder, 2012) – hard-hitting, funny and memorable – whatever genre you write.

Weiland, K.M., *Outlining Your Novel: Map Your Way to Success* (PenForASword Publishing, 2002) – not my scene, but some people swear by this.

Crime and its subgenres

James, P.D., *Talking about Detective Fiction* (Vintage; reprinted 2011) – an interesting overview from the modern Queen of Crime.

Rzepka, Charles, *Crime Fiction since 1800* (Polity, 2005)

Symons, Julian, *Bloody Murder: From the Detective Story to the Crime Novel* (Mysterious Press, 1993) – irreverent, but very entertaining.

Specialist handbooks

Gaute, J.H.H., and Odell, Robin, *Murder: Whatdunnit* (Pan, 1984) – this book is out of print and hard to come by now, but a wonderful sourcebook for writers in the genre. Sometimes available secondhand on Amazon. If you cannot get it, try Stevens and Bannon, below.

Lofland, Lee, *Police Procedure and Investigation* (Writers' Digest, 2007)

Lyle, D.P., *Howdunit Forensics* (Writers' Digest, 2008).

O'Byrne, Michael, *The Crime-Writers' Guide to Police Practice and Procedure* (Robert Hale, 2009)

Page, David W. *Body Trauma: A Writer's Guide to Wounds and Injuries* (Get it Write) (Behler Publications, 2006) – an American slant, but wounds are universal.

Stevens, Serita, and Bannon, Anne, *HowDunit: The Book of Poisons* (Writers' Digest, 2007)

Wilson, Keith D., *Cause of Death: A Writer's Guide to Death, Murder and Forensic Medicine* (Writers' Digest, 1992)

Wynn, Douglas. *Crime Writers' Handbook* (Allison and Busby, 2000) – a British compendium.

English language and usage

Joos, Martin, *The Five Clocks* (Harcourt, 1967) – the seminal and still the most approachable book on register. Usually available secondhand or in academic reprints. Have a look online.

Myers-Scotton, C. (ed.), *Codes and Consequences: Choosing Linguistic Varieties* (OUP, 1998) – a more modern take, all about register you'll ever want to know.

Phythian, B.A. *Essential English Grammar* (Hodder Education, revised edition 2010) – you have to know the rules to break them. If you're in any doubt try this, or any English as a Foreign Language usage and grammar book.

Truss, Lynne, *Eats, Shoots and Leaves: The Zero Tolerance Approach to Punctuation* (Profile, 2007) – an amusing handbook.

Memory and imagination

Baddeley, A.D. *Human Memory: Theory and Practice* (Psychology Press, 1994)

Hinton, G.E., and McLelland, J.L. *Neural Information Processing Systems* (American Institute of Physics, 1988) – a combined academic work by the chief fathers of 'parallel distributed processing' brain research. Not light reading.

Motluk, Roche, Cytowic et al., *Sweet Smell of Purple* (series of papers published in the *New Scientist*, August 1994 *et seq.*)

Advice and tips on writing crime from the United States

Frey, James N., *How to Write a Damn Good Mystery: A Practical Step-by-step Guide from Inspiration to Finished Manuscript* (St. Martin's Press, 2004)

Grafton, Sue (ed.), *Writing Mysteries* (Writers' Digest 2002) – an interesting collection of papers by different authors.

Ray, Robert J., and Remick, Jack, *The Weekend Novelist Writes a Mystery: From Empty Space to Finished Mysteries in Just 52 Weekends. A Dynamic Step-by-step Program* (Bantam Doubleday Dell Publishing Group, 1992)

Roerden, Chris, *Don't Murder Your Mysteries* (Bella Rosa Books, 2006)

Tapply, William G., *The Elements of Mystery Fiction: Writing the Modern Whodunit* (Poisoned Pen Press, 2004)

Wheat, Caroline, *How to Write Killer Fiction – the Funhouse of Mystery and the Rollercoaster of Suspense* (Perseverance Press, 2003)

Submission and presentation

Bingham, Harry, *The Writers' & Artists' Yearbook Guide to Getting Published* (A. & C. Black, 2010)

Whitelaw, Stella, *How to Write and Sell a Book Proposal* (Writers' Bookshop, 2000)

Also:

Morgan, Nicola, *Dear Agent: Write the Letter That Sells Your Book* and *Write a Great Synopsis* (both e-books, Crabbit Press (Nicola Morgan), 2013)

Finding an agent or a publisher

Cole, Martina (ed.), *Writers' & Artists' Yearbook 2014* (Bloomsbury, 2014) – now available as an e-book. Still the standard industry advice on all aspects of writing and publishing. Lists UK agents and publishers and includes helpful advice. The 2014 edition has a useful section on self-publishing and the Internet. This is one to keep. Get hold of the latest version (or download it) and update it every year or two.

Dyson, J. Paul (ed.), *Writers' Handbook: UK Directory 2014* (firstwriter.com, 2013 e-book only) – takes up where the *Macmillan Palgrave Writers' Handbook* seems to have left off, with comprehensive list of UK agents and publishers and what they handle.

Turner, Barry (ed.), *The Writers' Handbook Guide to Crime Writing* (Macmillan, 2003) – this appears to have gone out of print, though it is still currently available second-hand. Beg, borrow or murder to get hold of one. It lists all the UK agents and publishers who deal with crime and – though now a little out of date – will still save you hours of research.

In the United States:

Beck, Cathie, Klein, Amy, Thompson, John B., and Ferrari-Adler, Jofie, *Poets' & Writers' Guide to Literary Agents* (Poets and Writers, Inc., e-book only, 2014) – this is a new publication, though by a reputable organization.

Brewer, Robert Lee, *2014 Writer's Market* (Writers' Digest Books, 2013) – contains a lot of market information, including a short list of agents.

Sambuchino, Chuck, *2014 Guide to Literary Agents* (Writer's Digest Books, 2014; also available as e-book) – a yearly publication which gives up-to-date advice.

Self-publishing

There are large numbers of books, including some excellent free guides, about e-publishing. Look under Kindle, Smashwords, Googlebooks and similar.

Kindle is doing a series of handbooks you can buy and download, mostly by Bill McBride and Julie Wood, called 'Selling on Kindle Guides'. Naturally they are e-books. Or you might try the more general handbooks, such as:

Platt, Sean, and Truant, Johnny B. *Write. Publish. Repeat. The No-Luck-Required Guide to Self-publishing* (paperback, Realm and Sands, 2013; e-book, Stirling and Stone, 2014).

There are also companies who will do it for you for a fee.

Miscellaneous

Here are the titles and authors of the passages quoted in the Workshop exercise in Chapter 6.

Ian Rankin, *Knots and Crosses* (2008)

Mike Ripley, *Angel on the Inside* (2003)

Dorothy L. Sayers, *The Nine Tailors* (1934)

Andrew Taylor, *The Scent of Death* (2013)

Answers

Chapter 8, Workshop exercise

1 A bullock is a castrated bull.

2 Motorbikes don't generally have a reverse gear.

3 It isn't the flowers of monkshood which are poisonous.

4 A two-pound coin wouldn't be heavy enough to inflict a fatal injury.

Chapter 9, Snapshot exercise

Here is the passage again:

> When your looking through your manuscript for technical mistakes you might find it help to start at the bottom of the page – or the end of a chapter on a computer screen - and read upwards. Its earier to see errors when you aren't distracted by the sense. Highlight the errors as you go or note the line numbers on your jotter pad so you know were they are if you don't want to stop and correct them there and then. Don't make your technical edit til you've done any redrafting you want, or you'll have to do it again when the manuscript in it's final form.

And here it is, with typos and errors corrected. The amendments have been italicized, to highlight them. Alternative versions are given in parentheses.

> When *you're* looking through your manuscript for technical mistakes you might find *it a help* (or *it helps*) to start at the bottom of the page – or the end of a chapter on a computer screen – and read upwards. *It's easier* to see errors when you aren't distracted by the sense. Highlight the errors as you go(,) or note the line numbers on your jotter pad so you know *where* they are(,) if you don't want to stop and correct them there and then. Don't (*do*) your technical edit *until* (*till*) you've done any redrafting you want, or you'll have to do it again when the manuscript *is* in *its* final form.

You could also modify the register by amending contractions throughout, so 'you're' becomes 'you are' etc., and by changing 'Don't do' to something like 'delay', depending on the degree of formality you want.

Index

Index